The
LIVING
that
FULFILLS
GOD'S
ETERNAL
PURPOSE

WITNESS LEE

Living Stream Ministry
Anaheim, CA • www.lsm.org

First Edition, March 2004.

ISBN 0-7363-2760-6

Published by

Living Stream Ministry
2431 W. La Palma Ave., Anaheim, CA 92801 U.S.A.
P. O. Box 2121, Anaheim, CA 92814 U.S.A.

Printed in the United States of America

04   05   06   07   08   09   10   /   9   8   7   6   5   4   3   2   1

CONTENTS

PREFACE

This section is composed of messages given by Brother Witness Lee in Eugene, Salem, and Portland, Oregon, from June 4 through 9, 1963.

CHAPTER ONE

THE REALIZATION OF THE BODY LIFE

PUTTING OFF THE OLD MAN
AND PUTTING ON THE NEW MAN

Ephesians 2:15-16 speaks of the creation of the new man in Christ. These verses say, "Abolishing in His flesh the law of the commandments in ordinances, that He might create the two in Himself into one new man, so making peace, and might reconcile both in one Body to God through the cross, having slain the enmity by it." In verse 15 *the two* refers to the Jewish and Gentile believers, of whom the new man was created. Verse 16 indicates that this one new man is the one Body, that is, the Body of Christ, the church. According to these two verses the church is not only the one Body but also the one new man. There are not many new men; there is only one new man. Therefore, it is erroneous to consider that each believer is a new man. The new man is a corporate man composed of many persons. In the whole universe there is only one new man, and this one new man is the Body of Christ, the church.

Ephesians 4:22-24 reveals how this new man can be realized: "That you put off, as regards your former manner of life, the old man, which is being corrupted according to the lusts of the deceit, and that you be renewed in the spirit of your mind and put on the new man, which was created according to God in righteousness and holiness of the reality." First we must put off the old man, that is, the old Adam, the first corporate man; then we must put on the new man, which is to put on the Body of Christ.

To put on the new man is simply to realize the church, to have the genuine church life, which is the life of the new man, the life of the Body of Christ. The church life is realized by us when we put off the old man and put on the new man. Moreover, the secret to putting off the old man and putting on the new man is to be renewed in the spirit of our mind (v. 23). The more we are renewed in our mind by the spreading of our spirit into our mind, the more we will put off the old man and put on the new man, the more we will realize the church life, and the more we will realize the Body of Christ.

The new man is spoken of also in Colossians 3:9-11, which says, "Do not lie to one another, since you have put off the old man with his practices and have put on the new man, which is being renewed unto full knowledge according to the image of Him who created him, where there cannot be Greek and Jew, circumcision and uncircumcision, barbarian, Scythian, slave, free man, but Christ is all and in all." In the new man there cannot be any person other than Christ; He is all and in all. Since the new man is the Body of Christ, the church, in the Body of Christ there is nothing but Christ Himself. Thus, to have the church life is simply to have Christ Himself as our life. We realize the church life, that is, we put on the new man, simply by experiencing Christ in a genuine way.

First Corinthians 12:12 confirms this: "For even as the body is one and has many members, yet all the members of the body, being many, are one body, so also is the Christ." Here we see that Christ is not only the Head (Col. 1:18) but also the Body. Both the Head and the Body are Christ. Therefore, Christ Himself is the new man. He is both the Head of the new man and the Body of the new man. He is all-inclusive.

The way to realize the genuine church life is to experience Christ as life and as everything to us. God's eternal intention is for Christ to be wrought into us not only as our life but also as our everything. When we are regenerated, Christ enters into us and is born in our spirit to be our life. From that time on, God desires that we live by Christ (John 6:57; Phil. 1:21a), walk in Christ (Col. 2:6), and take Christ as everything to us—as knowledge, wisdom, light, energy, strength, power, and many other items (v. 3; 1 Cor. 1:30; John 8:12; Phil. 4:13; Eph. 6:10). This requires that we give up the old man, deny our self, and put off the old nature. The more we apply the cross to our old nature, our old man, the more we will experience Christ in a genuine way.

REALIZING THE ONENESS OF THE BODY

We need to be impressed that the church life is not a matter of doctrine; rather, it is Christ Himself realized by us in our daily life. We are the members of Christ. He is the divine vine, and we are the branches (John 15:5). We need to abide in Him and take Him not only as our life but also as everything to us. We need to live, walk, and do everything in Him, by Him, and through Him. Although we may know this already, it is one thing to know something, and it is another thing to realize it in our experience. Today there is much talk among the Lord's people concerning the problem of the unity of the church, that is, concerning the oneness of the Body of Christ. But the oneness of the Body can be realized only when we are living by Christ and walking in Him. The more we live by our self and walk in our self, the more sectarian we will be. In fact, all denominations and sects are formed because of one thing—human effort. If we deny our self and live by Christ, that is, if we put off the old man and put on the new man by putting on Christ as life and as everything to us (Rom. 13:14), there will be no need to talk about unity, because we will already be in the oneness of the church. The oneness of the church is nothing other than Christ experienced by us as the Spirit. It is not a matter of teachings. The more we talk about teachings, the more we will be divided, but the more we give up teachings and take Christ as everything to us, the more we will realize the oneness of the church.

The lesson of church history shows us that the more doctrines we have, the more we will be divided. However, the more we give up teachings and doctrines, live by Christ, put off the old man and put on the new man, and apply the cross of Christ in our daily life, the more we will be in the oneness of the Body. The urgent need today is for us to know Christ as life in a living and practical way. If we will practice this and be willing to apply Christ to our daily life by appropriating Him in all our daily matters, we will sense our urgent need to be one with other Christians. Teachings separate and divide, but life brings in oneness. When we are in Christ, taking Christ as our life and experiencing Him in a living way, we are in the oneness, because the reality of the oneness of the church is Christ Himself. It is not Christ in doctrines or teachings but Christ genuinely experienced by us as life that will bring us into the reality of the oneness of the church.

If we experience Christ in a real and living way, we will be in the church life and will never be individualistic. However, the more we work by our self for the Lord, the more individualistic we will be. If we give up the thought of serving the Lord by our self, if we simply deny our self, take Christ as our life and everything, and abide in Him, life will flow from within us. This flow of life brings in the oneness of the Body. The more we live Christ, the more we will long to be one with others, and the more we will be willing to be dependent on others.

If we experience Christ as everything, we will not be self-sufficient and thus become independent. On the contrary, the more we live by Christ, the more we will realize that we are just one member of the Body and that we can never be complete in ourselves. In our physical body each individual member needs the whole body, but a complete body as a whole does not need anything else. As a human being I am complete, with my own ears, eyes, hands, and feet. In a sense, I can be independent because I am a complete person. However, every member of my physical body needs to depend on the other members. Likewise, none of us is the complete Body; each of us is only a member (1 Cor. 12:14, 20; Rom. 12:5). However, if we live by our self, subconsciously we may think that we are complete and that we can be independent. If we live by Christ by denying our self and taking Christ as our life day by day, we will realize that we are nothing but a small member of the Body who needs the other members. When we are living in Christ, we long for the Body of Christ and for a relatedness between us and the other members. This is the genuine church life, and this can be realized only by the experience of Christ in our daily life. The church life can never be realized merely by teaching or by talking about the oneness of the church. Actually, the more we teach or talk about the oneness, the more we will be divided. The only way to realize the one-ness of the church is to experience Christ in a genuine way.

QUESTIONS AND ANSWERS

Question: Recently you gave us the main point of the books of 1 and 2 Chronicles, which is that no one can work by his own power, ability, or wisdom. Would you share something further about this?

Answer: We have to look at this portion of the Word with the view of the entire Scriptures, from beginning to end. The Scriptures reveal to us that God's intention in this universe is to have His house, His dwelling place, built up among the human race. The adamic race failed God in this matter, and God called Abraham in order to have a new beginning with a new race. The seed, the sons, of Abraham became the materials that God is using to build His dwelling place (cf. Gal. 3:26, 29). When the children of Israel came out of Egypt, God asked them to erect the tabernacle, which is a sign signifying that all the redeemed ones are a dwelling place for the Lord (Exo. 25:8; Heb. 3:5-6; Eph. 2:22). The tabernacle was a temporary dwelling place. The Lord's intention was that Israel would build a more permanent dwelling place, the temple, in the land of Canaan. The temple could be built up only through the victory of the children of Israel over all their enemies. Only after all the enemies had been defeated and terminated was it possible for the Lord to build up His dwelling place among His people. Therefore, before the building up of the temple could take place, there was first the need of fighting to remove all the enemies of God. In fulfilling this aspect of His purpose, King David was very much used by God. David fought the good fight for the Lord to put all His enemies to an end (1 Chron. 18—20).

Seemingly, David was the right person to build the temple. After he had gained the victory over the enemies, he himself thought of building a temple for God (2 Sam. 7:1-3). Nevertheless, God stopped him (vv. 4-16). Then, under the sovereign hand of God, David committed two serious sins. After he committed the first sin (ch. 11), he repented and confessed (Psa. 51). He received the Lord's forgiveness and obtained a son, Solomon, who was to build the temple (2 Sam. 12:13, 24-25). After David committed the second sin, he again repented and was forgiven, and he obtained a piece of land that would be the site for the temple (1 Chron. 21:1—22:1; cf. 2 Chron. 3:1). Moreover, during this period of his reign he prepared all the materials for the building up of the temple (1 Chron. 22:2-19).

Although the temple was built by man, it does not testify how much man can do for God. Rather, it testifies to the universe how much God can do for sinful mankind. However, the main thing we must see is that God's intention in all the generations of man is to build a dwelling place on this earth among the human race. This is the central thought in the Old Testament, which is primarily a history of the building of God's dwelling place. Indeed, the temple is the center of the Old Testament. Likewise, the center of the New Testament is the building up of the church as a dwelling place for God (Matt. 16:18; 1 Cor. 3:9-12a; Eph. 2:21-22; 4:12, 16). Eventually, the ultimate consummation of the entire Scriptures is the New Jerusalem as the eternal tabernacle and dwelling place of God (Rev. 21:2-3).

Therefore, in both the Old Testament and the New Testament God is building His dwelling place. In eternity God will gain a building as a temple, a dwelling place, for Himself. Our responsibility is to cooperate with God's building work. This is the reason that there is always a longing in the children of God for the church life. The more a person loves the Lord, seeks the Lord, walks in the Lord, and lives by the Lord, the more he longs to have a church life. This is something divine and of the Holy Spirit, not merely of ourselves, so that we may realize the church life and carry out the genuine building up of the church.

Question: How does this work in practice?

Answer: On the one hand, to carry this out in practice seems very complicated, especially in view of today's confusing situation. On the other hand, it is very simple. On the negative side, we must give up everything that is not of the Body. Just as our physical body rejects anything foreign to it, we must reject anything that is foreign to the Body of Christ. As living members of the Body of Christ, we know what is foreign to the Body and therefore does not belong to the church. On the positive side, when we are living in Christ, we will long to be related to others. To satisfy this longing, we must simply come together with others and take the ground as the expression of the Body of Christ in our locality. There is no need for us to study in a Bible institute. We simply need to give up all the foreign things and come together with those members who are available and take the ground as a local expression of the Lord's Body where we are. The Lord will bless and be with those who do this.

Furthermore, in our experience this is very workable. We should not think that we cannot meet together because we do not have a pastor or a church building. The way of hiring a pastor and building a church building is complicated and will not work. The simple way is the best. On the island of Taiwan there are many local churches, none of which was built up by a pastor or a full-time worker. Rather, all the churches in Taiwan were raised up by ordinary saints. We must forget about the foreign things and be simple. We should remember that we are believers, members of the Lord's Body, and come together with others in the simplest way. Then the Lord will be with us.

Question: What do you mean by the expression "learn to apply the cross in our daily lives"?

Answer: This simply means that we need to deny our self. The church is a new creation created by Christ, in Christ, and with Christ, and is actually Christ Himself realized within us (2 Cor. 5:17; Eph. 2:14-16; Gal. 6:15). Moreover, the new creation, as the new man, the Body of Christ, is Christ mingled with us (Col. 3:10-11). Hence, we must learn to deny the old life, which is the self, the adamic life, the old nature, the soulish life (Matt. 16:24-25). In the matter of denying the self, do not try to do anything by yourself, but simply accept what the Lord reveals to you. He will reveal clearly to you that your old life is finished, in other words, that you yourself are finished. Taking this ground, you can refuse to go along with your self and can simply take Christ as your life. In this way you will apply the cross to your daily life.

Question: Is there no need of struggling or discipline?

Answer: In the experience of the cross, the more we struggle, the more we turn the cross away from us. It is true that there is the need of discipline, but this is necessary only because we are too strong in either the mind, the emotion, or the will. Because of this, we need to be disciplined in order to be subdued. However, if we are always willing to give up our self, telling the Lord, "Lord, I am ready to give up my mind and my emotion in everything, and I will also pay the price to give up my will in everything," there will be no need for discipline. A test may come to us, but because we are willing to give up our self, there will be no struggle. It is simply because we are strong in our mind, emotion, and will that we struggle. The Lord has to discipline us again and again in order to subdue and break us so that we may be able to give up our self.

Many saints who seek the Lord are very much disciplined by the Lord because they are too strong in doing good for Him. They need to be broken in the matter of their doing good. It is not because they are sinful that the Lord disciplines them, but because they are good. The Lord has to raise up certain circumstances to press them, break them, and force them to give up their self. Only then will they be able to realize the oneness of the Spirit and the oneness of the Body. Indeed, we need to know that all the divisions and denominations were created by the best people; an evil person could never set up a sect, for no one would follow him. The more we are good, the more we will be independent, but the more we are spiritual and in the Lord, the more we will be dependent. It is one thing to be good, but it is another thing to be spiritual.

God's intention is for us to be God-men, not good men. A good man may not be a God-man; he may still be a soulish man. Only a God-man is spiritual (cf. 1 Cor. 2:14-15). Therefore, we must learn to give up our self in all things, not only in doing evil things but even more in doing good things, such as serving the Lord and working for Him.

Question: Is there any difference between what Watchman Nee proposes and what has been attempted by the Brethren?

Answer: Concerning the Brethren, there are two shortcomings in the way that they practice the church. First, they place too much emphasis on teaching and neglect life. Even when they teach concerning Christ, their teaching is mostly in dead letters. Merely to <u>have Christian teachings</u> <u>without</u> <u>realizing Christ Himself is</u> to <u>teach in dead letters,</u> <u>even if</u> <u>those teachings are concerning Christ.</u> It is Christ Himself as the Spirit whom we must realize, and any group of believers who meet together as an expression of the Body of Christ must be living and full of Christ. They must experience the reality of Christ. If all the saints experience Christ in a real and living way, automatically every problem will be solved and every argument will be terminated. According to our observation, among the Brethren there is too much teaching and very little reality of life.

The second shortcoming among the Brethren concerns the <u>basis of their meetings.</u> The meetings of the exclusive Brethren are narrow and sectarian. Although the open Brethren are more open to the Lord, they neglect the fact that there should not be more than one expression of the church in any locality. In a given city there should be only one local expression of the church, just as there was only one church in Jerusalem, in Antioch, and in Corinth, respectively (Acts 8:1; 13:1; 1 Cor. 1:2). In the New Testament there is <u>never more than one church in</u> <u>any locality</u> (Rom. 16:1; 2 Cor. 8:1; Gal. 1:2; Rev. 1:11), but the open Brethren have neglected this matter.

In some cities there are a number of open Brethren chapels. The different meetings are not called the church in that locality but are referred to as <u>local chapels on certain streets.</u> By holding such a practice, the open Brethren neglect the oneness of the Body in its local expression. Suppose, for instance, that on Twenty-first Avenue a group of Brethren saints are meeting together. After five months, three of the saints may no longer agree with the meeting because they have a difference of opinion. Hence, they may decide to leave the meeting on Twenty-first Avenue and begin another meeting on Eleventh Avenue. According to their practice, the first meeting will be called the Twenty-first Avenue Chapel, and the second, the Eleventh Avenue Chapel. Perhaps after another year has passed, a group of believers from the second meeting will divide and separate to meet on another avenue and begin another chapel. This illustrates the history of the Brethren in neglecting the oneness of the Body as expressed in localities. Although we have no intention of criticizing others, according to our realization of the truth in the New Testament, there must be <u>only one local expression of the Lord's Body</u> in each locality.

Question: Are you saying, in effect, that simply meeting in the name of the Lord Jesus Christ is not a sufficient ground, or a wide enough basis, for meeting?

Answer: In order to answer this question adequately, we need to review the history of the Christian denominations. Up to the time of the Reformation in the sixteenth century, there was the <u>Catholic Church</u>. In the <u>Reformation</u> the state churches came into being, which <u>were churches for the people but not of the people.</u> The monarchs became heads of their respective state churches. Hence, today the king of Denmark is the head of the Church of Denmark, and the queen of England is the head of the Church of England. After the state churches, the <u>private churches</u>, such as the <u>Presbyterian Church, the Baptist Church,</u> and the <u>Methodist Church</u>, came into being. These churches <u>were not only for the people</u> but also <u>of the people.</u> Then, in the early nineteenth century, through brothers such as John Nelson Darby, Benjamin Newton, and others, <u>the free churches</u> began. These churches were outside the denominations and organizations. Hence, today in Christianity there are the Catholic Church, the state churches, the private churches, and the free churches.

Since the time that the free churches began, Christians everywhere have claimed, on the basis of Matthew 18:20, that two or three believers meeting together constitute a church. This verse says, "For where there are two or three gathered into My name, there am I in their midst." The Lord, however, did not say that the two or three gathered into His name are the church. The conjunction *for* at the beginning of the verse indicates that what is spoken of thereafter is a continuation of something mentioned previously. Verses 15 through 17 say, "Moreover if your brother sins against you, go, reprove him between you and him alone. If he hears you, you have gained your brother. But if he does not hear you, take with you one or two more, that by the mouth of two or three witnesses every word may be established. And if he refuses to hear them, tell it to the church." According to the context, therefore, the two or three in verse 20 are the two or three witnesses mentioned previously in verse 16. They are not the church but are merely part of the church. If they have a problem, they should endeavor to solve it themselves. If they cannot, they must refer the problem to the church. The church in this chapter is the local church, not the universal church, for it is possible to "tell it to the church." This portion of the Word continues, "If he refuses to hear the church also, let him be to you just like the Gentile and the tax collector. Truly I say to you, Whatever you bind on the earth shall have been bound in heaven" (vv. 17b-18a). The church may bind the brother who refuses to hear the church, if the heavens have already bound him (cf. 16:19). Matthew 18:18b-20 continues, "Whatever you loose on the earth shall have been loosed in heaven. Again, truly I say to you that if two of you are in harmony on earth concerning any matter for which they ask, it will be done for them from My Father who is in the heavens. For where there are two or three gathered into My name, there am I in their midst." From all these verses it is evident that the two or three gathered into the Lord's name are not the church but are only certain members of a local church who are dealing with a brother who has sinned. There is no basis in the Lord's teaching in this passage for anyone to begin a meeting with just two or three in a home and call it a church. If in the same city you can have two or three meeting as a church in your home, and I can have two or three meeting as another church in my home, the church will be divided because of our failure to recognize the need to keep the oneness of the Body. In order to keep the oneness of the church in the locality where we are, we must be one with all the children of God in that locality. We must take the ground of the church in that place and stand as a local church.

Question: If we want to meet on the church ground, gather around the Lord's table, and be led freely by the Spirit, and if we extend open fellowship to all, but others do not come, where do we stand?

Answer: In today's situation everything is complicated and

confused, but we do not take responsibility for this. Rather, we must be responsible before the Lord for ourselves. If you see the light concerning the oneness of the church, you must practice it by the grace of God. Whether or not others would come is their responsibility. However, we must be careful of one thing: before beginning a meeting in any place, we must first find out if there are saints who are already meeting there and taking the ground of the church. If there are such believers, we must join them and submit ourselves to them. We should not start another meeting. If we are careless in this matter, we will do something wrong.

Question: Suppose there is such a group of believers, but some of the things they believe or practice are peculiar. How would you react?

Answer: It depends on how much these things damage the oneness. For instance, some believe in practicing foot-washing, whereas others believe in practicing head covering. These kinds of differences will not cause much damage to the oneness of the Body. To be sure, we cannot accept any difference that damages the oneness. However, when a difference concerns something that does not damage the oneness, when it is only a difference of thought, we need to be patient. The scriptural basis for this is Romans 14 and 15. In these chapters some saints insisted on eating meat, and others insisted on eating only vegetables. Some insisted on keeping certain days, and others considered every day the same. The apostle told them that they had to receive one another (14:1, 3; 15:7). His attitude was that those who keep certain days should not look down on those who do not, and that those who do not keep the days should not criticize those who do. He did not say what was right and what was wrong. He simply asked the saints to be patient with one another and receive one another. They had to accept all kinds of genuine believers.

Question: That would be a little hard to practice, would it not?

Answer: The matter of receiving the believers requires us to deny our self. For example, thirty years ago I saw the light that I should be baptized by immersion. From that time on, I would not agree with anyone who insisted on being sprinkled, and I refused to meet with such persons. Gradually, however, the Lord showed me that baptism by immersion is not what matters; what matters is Christ Himself. Having seen this, I can go along with those who insist on being sprinkled, as long as they love the Lord and live in the spirit.

The more we discuss matters of doctrine, the less we will be in the oneness. But if, instead of caring for differences in teaching and doctrine, we all learn to experience Christ in a genuine way day by day, we will be filled with Christ. Then we will forget about all the minor things. None of us will insist on anything, but we will bring everything to the Lord in fellowship to seek the Lord's mind. The Lord will lead us on. There will be no need to set up any regulation or observe any rule in the way of legality and dead letters. We should simply take Christ as our life and come together as a genuine local expression of the Body in the place where we are.

Question: How do you differentiate between coming together through Christ and knowing the will of Christ? Do you have to know the will of Christ in order to believe in this teaching?

Answer: To attempt to settle everything by means of knowledge through teaching is a dead practice. Instead, we need to take the Lord as everything and experience Him in a living way. Whenever anything happens, we need to come together to seek the Lord's mind by reading the Word, by prayer, and by fellowship. We do not need to set up any rules, but time after time and in a living way, we should simply take the living Lord with His living word for our experience. This will save us from the legality of dead letters and dead knowledge.

For example, it is a rule in dead letters to require the sisters to wear a head covering in the meetings. However, if we come together with the sisters to seek the Lord's mind by reading His Word and consecrating ourselves to Him to allow Him to speak to us, the wearing of a head covering will be something living. When we trust in the Lord and honor Him, He will lead us. Although a sister may never be subdued or submissive by our speaking to her concerning head covering, if we pray and seek the Lord with her, she may be very willing to take the Lord's word and command.

Question: Are you saying that even if what we teach is

scriptural, if a person receives it only because we said it and not because the Spirit revealed it, then that is of the flesh and not of the Lord?

Answer: We must realize that human beings love to set up certain rules, doctrines, and teachings and live by them. But in the New Testament the Lord never set up such things; rather, He gave some living teachings. Similarly, when they wrote the Epistles under the inspiration of the Holy Spirit, the apostles did not write in the way of setting up rules. Since this is the case, today we should not take the apostles' teachings and set them up as rules. What the apostles wrote were living words from the Lord, words that are fresh and refreshing, and today we must also have such fresh and refreshing words. Therefore, in everything we need to seek the Lord's mind together in a living way.

Question: How do we know where we are in the Body? How can we know our relationship to other members and how we fit in with the members in the Body?

Answer: The basic question we need to ask ourselves is, Do we really experience our Lord as life? If I live by my self and another member lives by his self, it will be very difficult for the two of us to fit in with each other. But if I live by the Lord and he lives by the Lord, it will be easy. When we come together, it will be easy to know where I am and where he is. Automatically and spontaneously, we will be fitted together in the experience of Christ as life. For example, I may not know whether I have the gift to minister the Lord's word. Nevertheless, I know because of the inward anointing that I have a measure of grace to do something in the Body. Through the anointing of the Holy Spirit each one of us has an inward assurance to know where we are, what we should do, and how we should be related to the other members. There is an inner feeling, sense, and assurance that comes from the anointing of the Holy Spirit within us. This is spontaneous.

What the Lord is seeking today is, first, that His people would experience Him as life in their daily living and, second, that He would have a genuine local expression of Himself in every locality. We are not saying that teachings are not necessary, but the urgent need today is for us to experience Christ as our life in a real way and then come together as a genuine expression of Christ in the place where we are. This is simple and effective. If we practice this, the Lord will be with us in everything we do.

Question: Have many great men had this vision?

Answer: According to our study of history, there have only been two occasions when the Lord's people endeavored to practice the church life in the genuine oneness. The first was with the Moravians under the leadership of Count Zinzendorf at the beginning of the eighteenth century. The second was with the British Brethren raised up by the Lord in the early nineteenth century. Apart from these two occasions, no other group intended to do this. For example, when the Baptists began to meet, they met not to have the church life but to maintain the truth of the proper baptism. The intention of the Presbyterians was not primarily to practice the church but to practice the Presbyterian system. Likewise, when John Wesley began a meeting, he did not have the light concerning the church. His intention was to practice holiness by a certain method, and this led to the name Methodist. Therefore, the attempt to practice the church life in the genuine oneness took place only on two occasions, the first of which was not as clear, full, or adequate as the second. However, today we believe that the Lord has taken a further step to realize the genuine expression of the Body of Christ in every place through the experience of Christ as life.

CHAPTER TWO

THE EXERCISE OF OUR HUMAN SPIRIT

THE THREE PARTS OF MAN

Concerning the creation of man, Genesis 2:7 says, "Jehovah God formed man from the dust of the ground and breathed into his nostrils the breath of life, and man became a living soul." In this verse three things are mentioned. First, God formed man from the dust of the ground; this was the forming of man's body. Second, God breathed into this body the breath of life, and third, man became a living soul. In this account of the creation of man, man's body and man's soul are clearly identified; however, it is not clear what the breath of life is that was breathed into man's body.

First Thessalonians 5:23 says, "The God of peace Himself sanctify you wholly, and may your spirit and soul and body be preserved complete, without blame, at the coming of our Lord Jesus Christ." This verse portrays man as having three parts: spirit, soul, and body. The body is the outermost part of man's being, the spirit is the innermost part, and the soul is the medium between the body and the spirit. In this verse the breath of life mentioned in Genesis 2:7 is clearly identified as the human spirit. This is confirmed by Job 32:8, which identifies man's spirit with God's breath.

The three parts of man correspond to the three realms in the universe: the physical realm, the spiritual realm, and the psychological realm. In the physical realm there are the material things, which we can contact through the body with its five senses of hearing, seeing, smelling, tasting, and touching. In the spiritual realm there is God, who is a Spirit (John 4:24). There are also the angels of God, who are spirits (Heb.

1:13-14); the enemy, Satan the devil, and the rebellious angels of Satan (Matt. 25:41), who are evil spirits; and the demons, who are unclean spirits (12:22, 24, 43). We can contact the spiritual world, in particular God as the Spirit, by means of the human spirit within us.

In order to contact anything, we need a certain organ to sense and substantiate it. For instance, it would be impossible to substantiate the sound of a voice without a hearing organ. If we were to lose the function of our ears, it would seem that the many voices around us did not exist, because we would have no organ that could substantiate them. Likewise, if we were to lose our sight, we could not substantiate color, and it would seem that such a thing as color did not exist. Although we might know that color exists, to our senses it would not exist, because we would not have the organ to substantiate color. This explains why unbelievers say that there is no God. To them there is no God simply because they have lost the function of their spirit. People who have lost the function of their spirit cannot substantiate God, because God is a spiritual being. We need to use the right organ to substantiate God, and that organ is our spirit. The Lord Jesus tells us in John 4:24 that "God is Spirit, and those who worship Him must worship in spirit." If we would know God, touch God, contact God, sense God, and substantiate God, we must use the right organ, that is, our spirit.

God created the stomach as the organ for us to receive food and water. In a similar way, He created the spirit as the organ for us to contact Him and receive Him. We would emphasize the fact that to sense and substantiate anything requires the right organ. For the physical world, God created our body with its senses, and for the spiritual world, in which God is the foremost item, He created a spirit within us. It is by this spirit that we can contact God. For this reason, when we pray, we need to stop our whole being and exercise our inner organ, that is, our spirit. We should pray not by our memory, nor by our mind, will, or emotion, but by the deepest and innermost part of our being, our spirit.

Many times we have experienced that the more we think and consider, the more we feel that the Lord is absent. If we exercise our mind and our reasoning too much, we may reach the point where we doubt that the Lord exists. But when we stop our whole being and exercise our innermost part, we sense the Lord's presence, because we are using the right organ to substantiate Him.

The soul is the medium between the body and the spirit. The word *psychology* comes from the Greek word *psuche,* which means "soul." Thus, psychology is related to the soul, and the psychological realm is the soulish realm. The soul is an organ by which we can sense and substantiate the psychological realm. Reasoning, anger, and joy belong to this realm. Both the Scriptures and our experience confirm that man is of three parts: spirit, soul, and body.

Hebrews 4:12 also speaks concerning the three parts of man: "For the word of God is living and operative and sharper than any two-edged sword, and piercing even to the dividing of soul and spirit and of joints and marrow, and able to discern the thoughts and intentions of the heart." This verse says that the soul and the spirit can be divided, showing that the soul and the spirit are not identical but are two separate parts of man. It also speaks of the joints and the marrow, which are parts of the body. It goes even further to speak of the heart with its thoughts and intents. The heart is different from the soul and from the spirit. Ezekiel 36:26-27 says, "I will also give you a new heart, and a new spirit I will put within you...And I will put My Spirit within you." In these verses three things are mentioned: a new heart, a new spirit, and God the Spirit. We need to differentiate between the soul and the spirit and also between the heart, on the one hand, and the soul and the spirit, on the other hand. Furthermore, verse 27 tells us clearly that God has put His Spirit within us.

TWO LIVES AND TWO MEN

When we received the Lord Jesus as our Savior, we were regenerated in our spirit. John 3:6 says, "That which is born of the Spirit is spirit." This proves that it was in our spirit that we were reborn, regenerated. When our spirit was regenerated, the Holy Spirit of God came into our spirit to enliven it and bring the Lord Jesus Christ into it as life. From that

Jesus 11:25 Jesus said to her, I am the resurrection and the life ; he who believes in Me, even if he should die, shall live .

John 14:6 Jesus said to him, I am the way and the reality and the life ; no one comes to the

Father except through Me .

time forward the divine life of God, the eternal life, has been in our spirit (Rom. 8:10). Our spirit was regenerated with the life of God by the Holy Spirit.

Before we were regenerated, we already had the human life. The human life is primarily the life of the soul. This is the reason that in the Bible men are called "souls" (Exo. 1:5, lit.; Ezek. 18:4). After God formed man's body from the dust of the ground and breathed into it the breath of life, a living soul came into existence. Man is a soul because the human life is mainly a matter of the soul.

Therefore, before we were regenerated, we were human beings with a human life mainly in the soul. The soul is the personality, the very self, of man, whereas the body is a vessel to contain the soul, and the spirit is an organ by which the soul can contact God. Before we were regenerated, we lived by the soul, by the human life, using the body as a vessel and the spirit as an organ. Now that we have been regenerated, there is another life in our spirit. This life is the divine, eternal life, which is Christ Himself (John 11:25; 14:6). Today we must realize that we have two lives: the human life in the soul and the divine life in the spirit. According to the human life in our soul, we are human beings and sons of men, and according to the divine life in our spirit, we are children of God and sons of God.

We have not only two lives but also two men, the old man and the new man. Ephesians 4:22 says, "Put off, as regards your former manner of life, the old man." We must put off the old man because it can never please God (cf. Rom. 8:7-8). It has already been condemned by God and put on the cross, crucified with Christ (6:6). Then Ephesians 4:24 says, "Put on the new man." These verses make clear reference to two men: the old man in the soul and the new man in the spirit. The old man has the human life, and the new man has the divine life. After our regeneration, our spirit is no longer merely an organ; it is a new man with the divine life. Hence, we must realize that we are persons with two lives and two men. We have the human life for the old man and the divine life for the new man. As Christians who are reborn children of God, our problem today is this: do we live by the human life or by the divine life, by the old man or by the new man? Herein lies the secret to the Christian life.

The Bible tells us that the old man has been crucified and that we must deny the self (Matt. 16:24; Luke 9:23). The self refers to both the old man and the soul. We need to deny the soul, and we should not live by the old man any longer, because the old man is condemned before God and has been crucified by the Lord on the cross. The "I," that is, the old man, has been crucified with Christ, and it is no longer this old "I" who lives, but it is Christ who lives in the new "I," the regenerated new man (Gal. 2:20). Our spirit is now a new man; hence, we must deny our self and live by the divine life in our spirit, which is to live by the new man.

We can know the difference between the soul and the spirit from our experience. The soul consists of three parts: the mind, the emotion, and the will (Prov. 2:10; Psa. 139:14; 1 Sam. 18:1; Job 7:15). We have a mind to think, to consider; an emotion to love and hate, to be happy and unhappy; and a will to make decisions and choices. These three parts together compose the soul. Many times as a Christian you may have considered doing a certain thing. According to your reasoning, it was right; it was also desirable, and eventually you made a decision to do it. In the process, you exercised all three parts of the soul: your mind to consider and reason about it, your emotion to like and desire it, and your will to decide on it. Yet at the same time deep within you there was a feeling against it. That was your spirit. This proves that there is something other than the mind, emotion, and will within us; there is something much deeper than the soul, and this is the spirit. By the soul, which has the human life, we can live as the old man. By the spirit, which has the divine life, the life of the Triune God, through regeneration, we can live as the new man.

TWO WAYS TO LIVE

How can we live by the divine life as the new man instead of by the human life as the old man? On the negative side, we must deny the old man, the soul, which means to deny the mind, the will, and the emotion. On the positive side, we must exercise our spirit, which means to exercise the deepest part of our being.

We can apply this principle to the matter of prayer. Many Christians pray by using their soul, not by exercising their spirit. Some pray by their emotion. When they are happy, they pray, "Lord, You are so good to me." Many others pray according to their memory, according to what they remember concerning their husband's business, their children, the church, and the gospel work. Instead of exercising their spirit, they exercise their mind to recite many things from memory.

In order to pray by exercising the spirit, we must forget about everything and come to the Lord to contact Him. For this we need to stop our whole being, including our memory, our thoughts, and our considerations. Then when we exercise our spirit, the Holy Spirit will work and move within us to energize us. At that time we will sense what the Lord's mind is, and we will not pray from memory but from our spirit.

Some sisters recite a certain set of prayers to the Lord day after day. Consequently, rather than feeling refreshed and satisfied within, they feel tired and grow weary of praying. However, if we pray by exercising our spirit, the more we pray, the more we will feel satisfied and refreshed. We will feel that we have been contacted by the Lord and that we have also contacted the Lord. From this we see that there are two ways to pray: by our mind or our emotion, and by our spirit.

The principle is the same with reading the Bible. There are two ways to read the Bible. Many read the Bible using only their mind. However, if we know how to contact the Lord, we will change the way we read the Bible. When we read a verse, we will exercise our spirit to digest it. For instance, after reading Genesis 2:7, we will immediately pray with our spirit to digest the verse. We may pray, "Lord, I praise You that You have created me with three parts. You have created a body for me, and also a spirit and a soul. Lord, I thank You for this body, through which I can sense and contact the physical world. And, Lord, I thank You even more that I can contact You because You are a Spirit and have created a spirit within me." In this way, we will exercise our spirit to eat the word. To exercise our mentality to understand and remember the word is tiresome, but to exercise our spirit to pray and to digest what we read strengthens, refreshes, and satisfies us.

The words in the Scriptures are spiritual food (1 Pet. 2:2; Matt. 4:4). In the matter of eating, what is important is not how much we understand but how much we take in. It would be foolish for me to ask someone what he understands concerning eggs, milk, meat, or lettuce. Instead, I need to ask him how many cups of milk he has taken in. To understand food is one thing, but to eat it is another. Likewise, to understand the word is one thing, but to take the word in, to eat and digest it by the spirit, is another. Jeremiah 15:16 speaks of receiving the Lord's words by eating them, and in the New Testament the Lord Jesus said, "Man shall not live on bread alone, but on every word that proceeds out through the mouth of God" (Matt. 4:4). The word of God is spiritual food that we must eat, not merely understand.

Furthermore, there are two ways to contact people. One way is to contact a person by our mentality or by our emotion. The other way is to contact the person by our spirit. In the morning while we are with the Lord, we may become burdened and very concerned in our heart and our spirit about a certain brother or sister. Then sometime during the day or in the evening we may contact that person not by our mentality or our emotion but by our spirit. This is the proper way to contact people.

Similarly, there are two ways to minister the word. One way is to use our mentality in knowledge, and the other way is by exercising our spirit. When we minister by our mentality, we can touch only people's mentality; we can never touch the spirit within them. But when we minister by exercising our spirit, our word will touch their spirit.

EXERCISING THE SPIRIT

Because we have two lives, the soulish life and the divine life, there are always two ways for us as Christians to do things. We can do things by the human life in our soul or by the divine life in our spirit. We can also act either as the old man or as the new man. The way to live for the Lord, following and obeying Him, is to not exercise our soul—our mind, emotion, and will—but to exercise our spirit. Our spirit is the innermost part of our being; it is deeper than our mind, emotion, and will. In order to live and walk by the spirit, we must learn to reject, to deny, the mind, the emotion, and the will. If we practice this, gradually we will realize that it is simple. Whenever we exercise a certain organ, it becomes stronger. Education teaches people how to exercise their mentality, but today we must realize that we need to learn how to exercise our spirit. Usually, when Christians come together, very few are strong in their spirit to utter a prayer or a praise to the Lord. Because they do not exercise their spirit in their daily life, they are very weak in their spirit. However, if we exercise our spirit day by day, our spirit will become positive, active, living, and strong. Then when we come to the meetings, it will be easy for us to express something either by giving a short word or by offering a prayer or a praise. Let us exercise our spirit to follow the Lord, to obey Him, and to live by and for Him.

To exercise our spirit, on the positive side, simply means to use our spirit. Our spirit is full of feeling and consciousness because the Holy Spirit is always working in our spirit. First John 2:27 says that the anointing which we have received from God abides in us. This anointing is not merely the Spirit as an ointment; it is the working and the moving of the Spirit in our spirit. The Holy Spirit as the ointment is always working, moving, and acting within us. The feeling of the anointing comes from this working and moving. Because we neglect the exercise of our innermost part, we do not take care of the inner feeling. But if we pay attention to our innermost part, we will sense that there is always a certain kind of feeling or moving, and we should go along with that feeling. This is the positive side of exercising our spirit. On the negative side, by exercising our spirit we will automatically deny our natural man, our natural way of thinking, our natural emotion, and our natural will.

If we exercise in this way, we will be normal Christians. The normal Christian life is a life lived in the spirit, where there is victory over sin, the self, Satan, the world, and worldly things. Some may say that we must substantiate our crucifixion with Christ through faith. However, all the things that the Lord has accomplished on the cross can be realized only in and through the Spirit, who dwells in our spirit. When we are in our spirit, all the divine facts that the Lord accomplished through His death and resurrection become real to us. If we are not in our spirit but in our self, it is not possible for us to experience what the Lord has accomplished on the cross. We need to walk in the spirit, which means that we must exercise our spirit.

DISTINGUISHING THE LIFE OF THE SOUL FROM THE FACULTIES OF THE SOUL

Furthermore, we must learn to distinguish the life of the soul from the faculties, or functions, of the soul. The soulish life must be put away, but the functions of the soul must remain. For example, if I am a clerk in an office, I must exercise the function of my mind; however, I should use my mind as an organ not by the life of the soul but by the life of the spirit. Then if my boss becomes unhappy with me, I can still work normally by using my mind as an organ. However, if I am living and working by the life of the soul and my boss becomes unhappy with me, I will become unhappy with him and will find it difficult to continue working normally. Therefore, as a clerk I must work by the organ of my mind, yet I should work not by the soulish life but by the life that is Christ Himself in my spirit. Since the natural man, the soulish life, has been crucified, we must reject and deny it; nevertheless, all the organs of the natural man still remain for us to use. To repeat, we must reject the soulish life but not the soul's faculties. Indeed, the more spiritual we are, the more we will function properly by the faculties of the soul.

We may also illustrate this by the love between a husband and a wife. The genuine love of a wife for her husband can be seen when the wife lives not by her own life but by her husband. She uses all her faculties but gives up her life in order to live by her husband. This is genuine love. As a husband, I know that to love my wife in a sincere way, I must always put my life aside in order to live by my wife. Divorces take place when husbands live by their own lives and wives live by theirs. Likewise, although God created us as independent human beings, He demands that we not live by ourselves but by Him. Moreover, although He created a life for us, He requires us to give up that life and take Him as our life. This is a wonderful matter.

The principle is the same with prayer. Genuine prayer is initiated from the spirit. When we come to the Lord in prayer, we must forget about our mind, emotion, and will and exercise our spirit. This affords the Holy Spirit the opportunity to burden us with certain prayers. Then automatically the human faculties of the mind, emotion, and will come into function. Sometimes as we come to the Lord, rejecting our mind, emotion, and will and exercising our spirit, the Holy Spirit energizes us within concerning certain matters, but our mind does not understand them. At such a time we need to pray, "O Lord, I simply do not have the utterance. Lord, be merciful; I simply do not know how to pray." It is at this time that the Holy Spirit in our spirit intercedes for us with groanings which cannot be uttered (Rom. 8:26).

Wherever I go, people ask me, "Brother Lee, please pray for me in this matter." I very seldom answer these requests affirmatively, because I am not sure whether the Spirit will lead me to pray in that way or not. I simply say, "If the Lord leads, I will do so." Genuine prayer is initiated not by us but by God on the throne. The Holy Spirit transmits to our spirit what the throne initiates, for us to sense as a burden in our spirit. If our mind has been transformed, it can interpret the burden in our spirit. When we utter that interpretation in words, we pray a genuine prayer, a prayer initiated by the throne of God and transmitted into our spirit.

Do not try to understand all these things thoroughly; it is impossible. The food we eat day by day can never be understood thoroughly. According to our experience, the simplest way to live the Christian life is to forget about our mind, emotion, and will and to exercise our innermost part to go along with the Lord. This is effective. For example, the more I think about a certain brother, the more unhappy I feel about him. This means that the more I exercise my mind concerning him, the more unhappy I feel about him in my emotion. But if I am following the Lord, I must forget about my mind and emotion and exercise my spirit to contact the Lord. I may pray, "Lord, I praise You. What should I do concerning this brother? In my spirit, Lord, energize me to love him." If we contact the Lord in such a way, our mind and emotion are still there, but something is different.

We can never explain this clearly or analyze it thoroughly, but it is nevertheless a fact. We must take the simplest way to experience this glorious fact. For our physical life, if we daily take milk, toast, and other good foods into us, we will receive the good things that we need in order to live, and day by day we will grow and be strong. The Lord Jesus said, "I am the bread of life...He who eats Me, he also shall live because of Me" (John 6:35, 57). The Lord is edible, and His desire is that we would eat Him. To eat the Lord is to exercise our spirit to contact Him. We must practice this. Our mind, emotion, and will must always be secondary, and our innermost part, our spirit, must always be primary. In all things in our daily life we must exercise our spirit to contact the Lord. Then we will experience the Lord in a real way and will be constantly energized by Him. If we continually exercise our spirit throughout the day, we will be holy. Sanctification will be ours, and victory over all things that oppose God will also be ours (Rom. 8:35-39). We will be spiritual and have power, energy, strength, light, and life because in our spirit we will experience all the riches of Christ. In the beginning we may feel that this is not simple, because we are not used to it. Learning to drive a car is awkward at the beginning, but after practicing for a time, it becomes easy. The Lord today is within us as life and as everything; hence, there is no need for us to struggle in order to be victorious, holy, or spiritual. We must exercise ourselves to apply the Lord to all the things in our daily lives. This is the way to be spiritual, holy, and victorious.

CHAPTER THREE

A CHRISTIAN LIFE
THAT FULFILLS GOD'S ETERNAL PURPOSE

THE RIGHT TRACK FOR THE LORD'S SEEKERS

In the beginning of this chapter I would like to consider the world situation as far as the Lord's interest is concerned. In many countries of Europe the situation is tragic. In France and all the southern European countries, from Portugal to Greece, there is nearly nothing for the Lord. I visited a number of places in Athens, Greece, but all that I found there was superstition. Concerning Scandinavia, there is something for the Lord in Norway, but it is very shallow. The Pentecostal movement in that country is quite prevailing, and it is better than in other places because it is not so wild. In Denmark, however, there is a deeper work for the Lord. In England, Scotland, and Ireland, although there was something for the Lord thirty years ago, the situation today is pitiful. When I was in Glasgow in 1958, a friend told me that in the district where we were staying, many people did not even know who Jesus was. There is still something for the Lord in England, but not as much as a century ago, when most of the important things of the Lord came from there. In Belgium, the Netherlands, Switzerland, and Germany, even though there are quite a number of Christians, there is not much at all for the Lord's interest.

From this we can learn something. Even though there have been revivals in these places throughout history, none of the revivals lasted very long. For example, even as recently as ten years ago there was a revival in Argentina, and thousands of people were brought to the Lord. But if you go there today, very little is left.

Furthermore, when I visited Turkey and some countries in the Middle East—Lebanon, Jordan, Israel, Iraq, and Iran—I discovered that there is nothing for the Lord's interest in these places. In the Far East, China has at least one-fifth of the world's population. In 1949 there were more than five hundred local churches there and approximately one thousand full-time co-workers. We planned to evangelize the whole of China in ten years, but suddenly, within the space of two years, the country fell into the hands of the enemy. Finally, it is difficult to find anything for the Lord's interest in Africa.

However, we praise the Lord that today throughout America there are many Christians, and among them a good number are genuinely seeking. They only need to be brought onto the right track. To be on the right track is, first, to know Christ and experience Him as life and everything, not in doctrine or teaching but in daily practice. Moment by moment we need to practice one thing, that is, to apply Christ and appropriate Him in all the events, situations, and conditions in our daily life. Second, to be on the right track is to come together with the seeking ones in the place where we live, without division or any sectarian spirit, to be nothing but "general" Christians. We should not be Presbyterian, Baptist, Methodist, or Lutheran, but just Christians in general, children of God, who are open to all the believers in Christ and who come together as a living, corporate expression of Christ. The right track, therefore, is to take Christ as our life and everything and then to meet with all the seeking ones purely as a living, corporate expression of Christ. This will bring much blessing from the Lord to His people. The Lord will honor this, and all the positive things that were lost during the past generations will gradually be recovered and experienced by us. We have the assurance that in these last days, before He comes back, the Lord will recover Christ as life and the church as His expression, not by a movement or a revival but by the fellowship of the Body of Christ and the current of life.

A CHRISTIAN LIFE
THAT FULFILLS GOD'S ETERNAL PURPOSE

In the Scriptures there are two different ways to approach

God's salvation. One way is from our side, and the other is from God's side. The first way is seen in the book of Romans. This book begins by revealing that we are all sinners under God's condemnation (1:18—3:20). Then it reveals Christ's redemption for our justification (Rom. 3:21—5:11). Following this, Romans reveals that not only our works and deeds are sinful, but even our nature, our very being, is sinful. We were all born in Adam, and there is nothing good in our flesh (5:19; 7:18). But this sinful man has been crucified on the cross with Christ (6:6), and now Christ as the Spirit lives within us (8:9-11). Furthermore, while we are walking, living, and doing things in the Spirit, we are members of one wonderful, universal, mystical Body (12:5). Therefore, we must have the Body life (vv. 1-21).

The book of Ephesians, however, is different. Whereas Romans begins with sinners, Ephesians begins with God. The starting point of Ephesians is in the heavenlies, not on the earth, and in eternity, not in time (1:3-4). This book shows us that in eternity past there was within God a desire, a good pleasure (vv. 5, 9). According to His good pleasure God made a purpose, a plan. This plan was made in eternity and for eternity, and thus it is called the eternal plan, or the eternal purpose. It is an eternal plan made in Christ, with Christ, through Christ, and for Christ according to God's desire and pleasure (vv. 9-11; 3:9-11). After God created all things, He called a number of people according to His selection and His predestination (1:4-5). He redeemed them, forgave them, and regenerated them to make them members of the Body of Christ (vv. 7, 13, 22-23). Now these people must be built up together as a living Body, a corporate vessel, to contain, express, and exhibit Christ to the whole universe (2:21-22; 3:20-21). For this they need to have the Body life (4:1—6:20). Therefore, although the two books begin differently, eventually Ephesians and Romans arrive at the same thing. Romans begins with sinners, and Ephesians begins with God in eternity and in the heavenlies. Both books reveal that God's plan, His intention, is to manifest and express Himself through Christ, His Son, in a universal, mystical Body composed of many created and regenerated persons. God needs an expression, one that is in Christ and through Christ, and also one that is through a Body of regenerated human beings. Without humanity, God can never be revealed or manifested, for man was created as a vessel for the purpose of revealing, expressing, and manifesting God (Gen. 1:26-27).

This is the reason that God created us with a mind with which to think, an emotion with which to love, and a will with which to make decisions. Without the human mind, God can never be revealed or expressed. Similarly, without the human emotion and will, God can never be manifested. Men were made as vessels for God (Rom. 9:21, 23; Acts 9:15). Many Christians today consider that we are instruments of God, but this is actually a wrong concept. There is a significant difference between a vessel and an instrument. A knife and a hammer are instruments, whereas a cup is a vessel. A vessel is a container. Romans 9:21 says that we are vessels of clay, and 2 Corinthians 4:7 says that we are earthen vessels that contain a priceless treasure. We are containers for Christ and for God.

As vessels we have a mind, a will, an emotion, and a heart. We may use a glove to illustrate this. In order to contain a hand, a glove must have five fingers, because there are five fingers on a hand. Likewise, God created us with a mind, an emotion, and a will because Christ has a mind, an emotion, and a will. The human mind is needed as a container for the mind of Christ, and the human emotion is needed as a container for Christ's emotion. First Corinthians 2:16 says, "We have the mind of Christ." If we did not have a mind, we could never have the mind of Christ. Therefore, our mind is a container for the mind of Christ, and our whole being is a vessel for Christ. We are not vessels for milk, eggs, or bread; we are vessels for Christ so that we might contain Him and express Him.

In order to express Christ, we were created by God according to Christ. Man was created in the image of God (Gen. 1:26), and Christ is the image of the invisible God (Col. 1:15). Hence, to be created in the image of God is to be created according to Christ. Just as a glove is made in the form of a hand so that it can contain a hand, we were created according to Christ so that we might be proper vessels to contain Him. Christ has a heart, and the heart within us is a container for the heart of Christ. Christ has a mind, and the human mind is a container for the mind of Christ. Christ also has a will, and the human will is a container for the will of Christ. Furthermore, we are vessels not merely to contain Christ but also to be filled with Him so that He may be formed in us (Eph. 3:17, 19; Gal. 4:19). We may put a hand in a glove, but the hand may not be formed in the glove. Only when every finger has been fitted exactly inside the glove can we say that the hand is formed in the glove. Christ may be in us but not yet formed in us. We need to be filled with Christ, and Christ must be formed within us.

We need to be impressed that God created the universe in order for Christ to be expressed through His Body. All the things on the earth and in the heavens, with man as the center (Zech. 12:1), are for the purpose of expressing Christ through His Body. This is also the reason that God selected us as the object of His divine grace. He needed us to be a Body to contain, express, and exhibit Christ to the whole universe.

ENJOYING CHRIST AS THE REALITY

Now let us consider who Christ is as the content of the vessel. Christ is the mystery of God (Col. 2:2). Without Christ, God is truly a mystery, and no one can understand Him. If you ask unbelievers, even those with Ph.D. degrees, what the meaning of the universe is or what the meaning of human life is, they will tell you that they do not know. Although they may be very knowledgeable concerning science and philosophy, the meaning of the universe and of human life remains a mystery to them. God is a mystery, but Christ is the explanation, definition, and expression of this divine mystery. If we have Christ, we understand the mystery, and we know the meaning of the universe and also of human life. Today Christ as the very mystery is within us as life (3:4). For the present He is our life, and for the future He is the hope of glory (1:27). He is our portion (v. 12), and we are partakers of Him. Daily we experience and enjoy Him as our food, drink, light, life, peace, patience, joy, and everything.

We need to realize that all the material things around us are not the reality but are only shadows (2:16-17). The chair we sit on is not the real chair. The three meals we eat day by day are not the real meals. They are only figures, types, or symbols that signify and point to something real, that is, to Christ as our real life (John 14:6) and our real food (6:48). Moreover, the light in a building is not the real light. Although we may be in a room with a very intense light, without Christ we are still in darkness, because the physical light is only a figure that denotes the real light, which is Christ as the light of life (8:12). Christ is not only food and light to us; He is also a house as our dwelling place. In Psalm 90:1 Moses said, "O Lord, You have been our dwelling place / In all generations." At the time Moses said this, he was between eighty and one hundred twenty years of age. As an old man he knew that every material thing was not trustworthy and that the eternal habitation of God's people is the Lord Himself (Rev. 21:22). We must take Christ as our abode and live in Him as our dwelling place (John 15:4). Christ is everything to us. He is our life, our food, our drink, our light, our way, our wisdom, our knowledge, our strength, and our power (Col. 3:4; John 6:35; 4:10, 14; 7:37-39; 8:12; 14:6; 1 Cor. 1:24; Col. 2:3; Phil. 4:13). Christ is also our authority (2 Cor. 10:8; Rev. 2:26), our Husband (2 Cor. 11:2), our Brother (Rom. 8:29), and our Father (Isa. 9:6). Therefore, all the physical, visible things are merely signs and figures of Christ, who is our portion and whom we should enjoy, experience, and partake of moment by moment.

When we receive Christ as our Savior, God reveals Him into us through the Holy Spirit (Gal. 1:15-16). This matter is wonderful and mysterious, but regrettably, many Christians who are genuinely saved do not know that Christ has been revealed into them and is now within them. Thus, when they pray, they think that Christ is in the third heaven, far above and beyond them. However, mysteriously, the more we pray, the more we feel that the Lord is here, within us. Christ has been revealed into us, and He is waiting for us to take Him as our life.

We also need to realize that as regenerated Christians we have two lives, the human life and the divine life. Every

Christian has been born twice; first, he was born of his parents to have the human life, and then he was born of God through the Holy Spirit to have the divine life, which is Christ Himself (John 1:12-13; 3:6; 11:25). The problem today is this: What life do we live by? Do we live by ourselves or by Christ, by the human life or by the divine life? Since we have been crucified (Rom. 6:6), we must apply the cross of Christ to our human life (Matt. 16:24; Luke 9:23). This means that we must always take the standing that we have been crucified on the cross. In other words, we are finished, put to an end. It is because of this fact that when we receive Christ as our Savior, we are baptized into water. As crucified persons, we are dead; hence, we must be buried (Rom. 6:4; Col. 2:12a). Often I tell candidates for baptism, "Baptism is a funeral, and to be baptized is to be buried. You have believed in Jesus Christ, but now you must know that when Christ was crucified on the cross, you were included in Him. This means that you too have been crucified. Because you are a dead person, we cannot keep you here any longer; we must bury you." We are crucified, and it is no longer we who live, but it is Christ who lives in us (Gal. 2:20). Christ is our life, and we must live by Him, not by our self. Whenever we are going to live by our self, we must tell ourselves that we are buried in the tomb, and thus it is wrong for us to continue living.

Furthermore, Christ must be formed within us (4:19). For this we must be transformed into Christ's image (2 Cor. 3:18) and conformed to Christ (Rom. 8:29). Then when we consider something, we will consider it in the same way that Christ does; when we love someone or something, we will love in the same way, manner, attitude, and atmosphere as Christ loves, and in our love we will sense the taste of Christ; and when we decide something, it will be Christ's decision, for there will be the element of Christ in our decision. This is to have the image and form of Christ.

In this chapter we have covered the first aspect of the Christian life that fulfills the eternal purpose of God. On the one hand, Christ is our portion, and we enjoy Him day by day. On the other hand, Christ is the image that must be formed in us, and we must be conformed to Him. Our whole being must be saturated by and with Christ so that we are transformed into His image. According to human experience, nothing but Christ can fully satisfy us. But we must experience Him in a very practical way. We need to have Christ not just in teaching, theory, or doctrine but in our practical daily life. We need to appropriate Christ in our daily life by enjoying Him moment by moment, experiencing Him and applying Him to all that happens in our daily living. This is the Christian life, and this is the only life that can satisfy us. If we are living such a life, day by day we will be full of peace, satisfaction, and joy. This is the individual aspect of a life that fulfills God's eternal purpose. In the next chapter we will cover the corporate aspect.

QUESTIONS AND ANSWERS

Question: How can we apply Christ as you have described?

Answer: Applying Christ is very simple. We can compare it to turning the lights on by turning a switch on. Before the lights in a building can be switched on, electricity must be installed in the building. Then whenever we need light, we can simply turn the switch on. We have been regenerated by the Holy Spirit with Christ, which means that Christ has been installed in us. Now He is within us, and the only thing we need to do is to switch on.

Question: What if we "blow a fuse"?

Answer: Sometimes we lose our temper, and as a result, we "blow a fuse." When this happens, we must confess our sin and get connected again. We must confess our weakness and be cleansed by the blood of the Lord Jesus. According to 1 John 1:1-9, when we receive the divine life, the eternal life, we also have the fellowship of the divine life. This fellowship may be likened to the current of electricity. There is a current of the divine life, and this current is the fellowship. Christ Himself is the electricity, and the fellowship is the current. When we confess our sins, the blood of Jesus the Son of God cleanses us from all defilement and recovers the lost fellowship (vv. 7, 9). Then, once again we are in the current of the divine life.

Question: Should we hope for a mighty work of the Spirit in these days before the Lord returns?

Answer: This is a traditional Jewish concept. Judaism has always told people that one day the late rain will come (Hosea 6:3), in other words, that there will be a great revival. However, although for many centuries people have been talking about the late rain, the anticipated revival has still not come. Nevertheless, from the past centuries up to the present the Lord has done many things not in the way of a revival but in the way of life.

Consider, for example, a farm with its crops. Although there is no revival, all the plants that bear fruits and vegetables are quietly producing day by day. This is the power of life, and this is what we need. I have witnessed many meetings in which people shouted, cried, and even claimed to have a holy laughter. However, it was difficult to find any evidence of genuine power among them. Genuine power is certainly not in shouting, rolling, laughing, or jumping; rather, it is in Christ. When we experience Christ, even silently, we are full of power, because the real power is Christ Himself. The apostle Paul told the Corinthians, "For indeed Jews require signs and Greeks seek wisdom, but we preach Christ crucified." To those who are called by God, this crucified Christ is "the power of God and the wisdom of God" (1 Cor. 1:22-24). Signs are miracles, manifestations of power, which the Jews sought after. But the apostles did not preach miracles and signs, nor did they preach wisdom and knowledge. Rather, they preached Christ crucified. The crucified Christ is both the power of God and the wisdom of God. Thank the Lord that in century after century there has been the current of life, that is, the current of Christ, and many people have been brought to God through the saving power of Christ as life. The experience of Christ in our daily life is something divinely powerful. Christ as life is real power, but He must be daily experienced by us as our portion and enjoyment (Col. 1:12).

Question: How are the inner sense and the working of Christ related?

Answer: If we would enjoy and experience Christ, first we must be very simple. Teachings and doctrines complicate our experience of Christ. Then we must realize that Christ the Lord is within us (Rom. 8:10; 2 Cor. 13:5), and He lives, acts, moves, and works in us unceasingly. Thus, there is always a certain kind of sense, feeling, or consciousness within us, and we must simply go along with that sense. We should not decide to please God. We can never please Him, because we are good for nothing except to be buried. Since we are in the tomb, why should we come out of the tomb and try to please God? Neither should we attempt to work for God. In the Gospel of John the Lord Jesus said, "Abide in Me and I in you...I am the vine; you are the branches...Apart from Me you can do nothing" (15:4-5). There is no need for us to do anything good. We should simply abide in Christ according to the inner, living sense of the divine life within us. We should go along with that sense and should abide in Christ according to that sense. Then Christ will energize and strengthen us to do many things, and it will not be we who do those things; it will be Christ who does them in us (Phil. 4:13). In this matter we must beware of the enemy Satan's strategy. At a certain time we may not love the Lord and may frequently lose our temper. When we return to the Lord and begin to love Him again, immediately the enemy will come in and tempt us to make the decision never to lose our temper again. Eventually, however, we will discover that the more we endeavor to control our temper, the more we will lose it. Therefore, we must change our concept from trying to please God to gaining Christ (3:8). Christ is real, and He is living within us. Therefore, we need to be simple and apply Him.

Question: I know that for you this concept has become a reality, but to me it is still only a theory. Is this something that develops with the Lord over several years?

Answer: To analyze our experience in this way is to be too much in the realm of mental consideration. We need to learn to give up our mentality and simply be in the spirit. For example, I can know a great deal about electricity, but if I do not turn the switch on, I will still not have electricity. Similarly, there is a great difference between a menu and the meal itself. Even to have a meal set before us is not the same as actually eating it. Christ is within us; He is real and living. The Lord Jesus said, "He who eats Me, he also shall live because of Me" (John 6:57). To eat Christ day by day is to apply Christ to our daily living. Christianity and even Christian teachings are not the same thing as Christ. Christ Himself is what counts. We are not concerned with a religion of dead letters or even with Christian teaching, but rather with Christ Himself as the living reality. The most urgent need among the Lord's people today is not more teachings; it is the real application and the living realization of Christ.

Question: Should we learn part of the Word and then act on it so that it becomes part of us?

Answer: We must convert our knowledge of Christ into prayer. In this way we transfer our knowledge from the mind to the spirit, and then the knowledge of the Word becomes living food to us. Among Christians today there is too much knowledge, too much exercising to read, study, hear, and listen; in other words, there is too much exercise of the mind and very little exercise of the spirit.

Question: When we see something of Christ in another believer, can that pattern communicate Christ to us?

Answer: Whether or not we receive Christ through the pattern of another believer depends on our prayer. To pray is to contact the Lord. If we are truly influenced by the patience of Christ expressed in a certain brother, we must go to the Lord and say, "Lord, I praise You that here is such a brother who is full of Yourself. Lord, I would like to be filled with You, as he is." When we pray in this way, we will touch the current of the spiritual life within us. This is the real fellowship and prayer. As we are living and working in the Lord, we can talk to the Lord. Whether or not we receive an answer to our prayer is secondary; contacting the Lord is the primary matter. Real prayer is not to ask the Lord Jesus to do something for us; real prayer is to contact the Lord and absorb Him. Then we will live a life that is spiritual, sanctified, and victorious.

CHAPTER FOUR

GOD'S PLAN TO WORK CHRIST INTO US

Prayer: Lord, we look to You that You would open to us Yourself with Your Word. You are our Father, and we are Your children. We come to You with a sincere heart, a seeking spirit, and an open mind to seek You so that we may receive mercy and find grace for timely help. Lord, we do express to You our longing heart. How much we need You and the covering and cleansing of Your precious, prevailing blood. Even more, we need You as the anointing to us. O Lord, we commit ourselves into Your hand. May these days be full of light and life that we may be brought into Your vision to see something heavenly and eternal. Do something definitely in these days, not for us but for Yourself, Your testimony, and Your recovery. By Your headship and lordship we claim all the seeking saints for the recovery of the testimony of the church in these last days. Lord, we praise You because we have the assurance that You are moving in a deeper way and in a mighty way. We trust in You for everything that You have committed to us. We say today that we are nothing; we are impotent and incompetent, but we trust in You and put our confidence in You. At this very moment cover us, head us up in Yourself, and fight the battle for Your kingdom. We pray, Lord, that You will bind the strong man, the enemy, to release what is Yours from his hand. We ask this in Your name. Amen.

THE NEED TO SEE GOD'S ETERNAL PLAN

In these messages we are covering the line of Christ as life and the church, the Body of Christ, as the expression of Christ. These two items are the urgent need today. As Christians, as reborn ones, we must see God's revelation concerning His eternal purpose. There must come a day when we definitely see that in this universe God has a divine plan, an eternal plan, which He made in eternity and for eternity. If we do not see this, we will be Christians whose condition is below the divine standard. In order to be up to the standard, we must see the eternal plan revealed to us in the whole of the Scriptures.

In man there is a natural concept concerning God and the divine things. When we were sinners, we had no heart for God and no thought about God. We did not care for the divine, spiritual things; on the contrary, we were very much occupied by the worldly, sinful things and the desires of the flesh (Eph. 2:1-3; Titus 3:3). However, when we turned to the Lord, immediately we exercised our natural understanding to comprehend and apprehend the divine and spiritual things. We may think that our natural understanding is right, but we must realize that it is absolutely wrong. Although the natural concept seems good, it is very dangerous and is a great hindrance to our seeing God's eternal plan.

When a person repents, that is, when he turns his mind toward the Lord, immediately he has many concepts. First, since the Lord has been good and gracious to him, he feels that he owes the Lord a great debt. Second, he decides to love the Lord and is willing to even sacrifice his life for the Lord. Third, he decides to read the Scriptures because he feels that there are many things he needs to know and to keep. Fourth, he decides to do only good things and to adjust and correct himself as a new man. Last, he may even decide to serve the Lord in the church or preach the gospel. Whenever a person turns to the Lord, he will naturally have concepts like this. However, such concepts are not of the Lord. To hold such concepts is to be taken advantage of by the enemy, who would hinder us from knowing the Lord in a real and spiritual way.

COOPERATING WITH GOD FOR HIS PLAN

The Lord has a plan, and the center of this plan is that God in Christ as the Spirit desires to mingle Himself with us. The carrying out of God's plan requires our cooperation. We were created as vessels for God, but God did not create us as vessels without life, feelings, intentions, desires, or understanding.

We were created as living vessels. To fill a glass with water is easy because the glass is without any understanding, desire, thought, or intention. Thus, it is easy to deal with. However, as all parents know, to give medicine to a child is rather difficult. Sometimes parents need to grasp a young child and hold his mouth open before they can give him medicine. This is necessary simply because the child is living. He has his own intention, thought, and desire, and he does not want to cooperate with his parents. God made us as living vessels, but when He comes to fill us with Himself, many times we do not cooperate with Him.

The most glorious and pleasing thing to God is our cooperation with Him in allowing Him to fill us with Himself. Sooner or later we will discover that we are persons who are willing to act by ourselves in doing many things for God, but we are not willing to cooperate with God. Often in the past forty years I had a desire to do things for God. Yet in my innermost being I had the sense that I should stop and open myself in order to give Him the cooperation so that He might come in, occupy me, and fill me. Truthfully, although I knew I should do this, I did not have the intention or the desire to do it. I was like a child who knows he should take his medicine but has no desire to do so. A child would rather do many things for his parents than cooperate with their demand to take his medicine. This is our real condition before God. We like to help people, preach the gospel, and do many things for the Lord, but as we are doing these things, deep within us there is a sense that we must stop ourselves from our doing, open ourselves to cooperate with the Lord, and let the Lord operate on us.

BEING STOPPED TO RECEIVE REVELATION

We Christians always try to do things and work for the Lord, but the Lord wants us to eat Him and drink Him by enjoying Him and feeding on Him. We should not be "doing" Christians but should be "eating" Christians. We should not be "working" Christians but "drinking" Christians. We need a revelation that God's eternal purpose, His ultimate intention, is to mingle Himself with us and work Himself into us. This is the divine thought. Once we have this thought, our concept, nature, conduct, and even our whole being will be changed, transformed, and revolutionized.

Even though I have made many mistakes and committed many sins, the things I have repented for the most before God are not my mistakes and sins but the things that I tried to do for the Lord. When I do not have light, I think that I must do this or that for the Lord to work for Him and serve Him. But once I receive light, I know that I am on the wrong track and am not going along with the Lord. At such a time I sense that I must cease from my doing, working, and serving and give the Lord a chance to work on me and in me. I need to prostrate myself before the Lord, asking Him to forgive me for doing such foolish things. We need to be delivered from doing, from working, and from serving God. On the one hand, we encourage people to exercise to give testimonies or offer prayers in the church meetings. On the other hand, we know that there will be a time when the Lord will reveal to such people that they must stop from exercising anything and be delivered from all kinds of activities. If we are sick, in order for the doctor to operate on us, we must submit ourselves to him. This simply means that we stop ourselves from doing, from working, and from any kind of activity and offer the doctor our absolute cooperation.

During the years from 1938 to 1943 I was working so much for the Lord that no one could stop me. The more I worked, the more the work interested me. Yet there was a deep sense within me that I should stop a little. It seemed that the Lord was saying, "You need to stop. Do not work so much for Me. Let Me work on you, and let Me work in you." Nevertheless, because I would not listen to this inner sense, the Lord came in and disciplined me. First, He put me in prison, and then He put me in a sickbed for more than two and a half years. This was not because I had committed some sins but simply because I did too much for the Lord. The Lord needed my cooperation. Since I would not stop, He made me lie down. During those three years, more and more revelation came to me as I repented for my doing too much for the Lord.

We have pointed out that the Lord's eternal purpose is

to work Himself into us. Strictly speaking, we are not the workmen or the workers; rather, we are the work, the workmanship, of the Lord (Eph. 2:10), and we must be worked on by the Lord. Do not think that we need to work for the Lord. If a piece of building material tried to work for the builder, he might tell it, "Stop. Let me work on you. Only after I have worked on you will you be useful for my purpose. The degree to which you will be useful for my purpose depends on the degree to which you are willing to be worked on by me. Only in this way can my building be accomplished. The more active you are, the more you hinder me from building." Sooner or later, if we have a sincere heart in seeking the Lord, He will stop us from our doing and reveal to us that we need Him to mingle Himself with us and work Himself into us.

BEING FILLED, PERMEATED, AND SATURATED WITH GOD HIMSELF

After being regenerated, many Christians become like Saul of Tarsus, doing what he did before he was regenerated. Whereas the apostle Paul was Saul before he was regenerated, we are "Sauls" after our regeneration. Saul was very active in working, moving, and doing things in Judaism (Gal. 1:13-14; Phil. 3:4-6). One day the Lord met him in order to stop him from his doing and blind him. Before that time he always took the lead to move and to act, but after the Lord met him, he needed someone to lead him (Acts 9:1-9). From that day forward God revealed His Son in Saul (Gal. 1:15-16). God showed him that what He wants is not human activity but a human vessel who is willing to cooperate with God's desire to fill him with Himself (Acts 9:15). God wants to fill us with Himself; He wants to enter into us to saturate us with His element and permeate us with all His riches. For this, He needs our cooperation. Everything of the Christian life, the Christian service, and the church life must come out of this. We may have been a Christian for many years, but even today we may not have seen the eternal plan of God.

The revelation of God's eternal plan will stop us from all kinds of activities. We will prostrate ourselves before God and open ourselves absolutely to the Lord, saying, "Lord, I hate my doing, I hate my service, I hate my work, and I hate all the good things that I do. I hate these more than I hate the sinful things, because they are stronger hindrances to Your coming in to fill me, Your saturating me with all Your fullness, Your permeating me with Your element, and Your mingling Yourself with me. Now I know that Your purpose is not a matter of my doing or my working but a matter of Your filling me with Yourself." This is the eternal purpose of God. All the divine and spiritual things must come out of God's mingling Himself with us.

The heart of many Christians is toward the worldly things rather than toward the Lord. Nevertheless, there are a good number of Christians who have been saved and who have a sincere heart and desire to seek the Lord. Some of them endeavor to serve the Lord by consecrating themselves to be missionaries on foreign fields. Some endeavor to do good, and some are seeking the deeper life, the victorious life, the holy life, the crucified life, the spiritual life, or the Christ-centered life. Furthermore, there are some who insist that we must experience the baptism in the Holy Spirit and speak in tongues. Some believers stress absolute grace, others teach Arminianism, and still others espouse Calvinism. However, once we see God's eternal purpose, all these things disappear. When the sun is shining, there is no need of the stars. When we see God's eternal purpose, the only thing that counts is God mingling Himself with us by working Christ into us. As long as we cooperate with God to have Christ wrought into us, we will have the deeper life, the holy life, the victorious life, the sanctified life, the crucified life, and the spiritual life. We will also be prevailing and powerful in our prayer and service, and we will be full of life in our work and in our daily living. This is the central point. The centrality and universality of everything is for Christ to be wrought into us.

Today there are many things that believers emphasize. Some emphasize prayer and intercession, urging us to pray seven times a day as David the king did (Psa.119:164). Others insist that we must study the Scriptures by attending a Bible institute or seminary. However, neither of these is the answer. The answer is Christ Himself as the center and as everything, not in doctrine, in teaching, or in knowledge but in experience, in practice, and in reality. What we need today is the living experience of the living Christ as the living Spirit (1 Cor. 15:45; 2 Cor. 3:17). Our need today is a living person, Christ Himself, experienced and enjoyed by us day by day. Then we will know what the central thought of God is.

QUESTIONS AND ANSWERS

Question: Galatians 6:2 says, "Bear one another's burdens, and in this way you will fulfill the law of Christ completely." How and in what attitude should we bear one another's burdens, and what is the law of Christ and its fulfillment?

Answer: Suppose you were to ask a peach tree that bears peaches, "Please tell me what it means to bear peaches." If the tree could speak, it might answer you, "I do not understand how to bear peaches, but I do understand how to live by receiving many kinds of supply from the soil, from the water, from the wind and the air, and from the sunshine. As long as I live by all these things, I will spontaneously bear peaches." The verse concerning bearing one another's burdens is in the sixth chapter of Galatians, not in the first chapter. In the first chapter Christ is revealed in us (vv. 15-16), in the second chapter Christ is living in us (v. 20), in the third chapter Christ is our clothing (v. 27), in the fourth chapter Christ is formed in us (v. 19), and in the fifth chapter we are not separated from Christ (vv. 4-6). If this is our condition, we will surely bear the fruit of the Spirit.

Galatians 5:22-23 speaks of fruit, not of fruits. What is mentioned in these verses should not be considered nine kinds of fruit, but one kind of fruit with nine aspects. The first aspect of the fruit of the Spirit is love, and the last aspect is self-control. Toward others we must always have love, and in dealing with ourselves, we must always have self-control. These are the aspects of Christ as life, and they are an overflow of the Christ whom we have experienced. When we experience and enjoy Christ, He will flow Himself out; this outflow is the fruit. Christ is the fountain of the flow of life. If we abide in Him and allow Him to abide in us, there will be an outflow of life from within us, which is the fruit of the Spirit, with love as the first aspect. The law of Christ in chapter 6 is the law of love, which is substantiated by the law of the Spirit of life (Rom. 8:2). The law of love enables us to bear one another's burdens. Then at the end of the book the apostle tells us that neither circumcision nor uncircumcision is anything, but a new creation is what matters (Gal. 6:15). Human morality and human immorality, human good and human evil, do not mean anything. None of these things avails, but a new creation is what matters. A new creation is a person who is mingled with Christ, a person who has Christ revealed in him, Christ living in him, Christ covering him as his clothing, Christ being formed in him, and Christ being a fountain of life within him. To repeat, neither doing good nor doing evil avails before God. These things are nothing. What is needed is a new creation, which comes into being through our being mingled with Christ. This is the right position and condition for us to have.

Question: How can we abide in Christ?

Answer: In order to abide in Christ, at least once we need to see that we are in Christ. This is a fact. We are persons who have been put into Christ by God (1 Cor. 1:30). Thus, we are in Christ. To abide in Christ simply means to not go outside of Christ but to keep ourselves in Christ. There is no need for us to strive to be in Christ, because we are already in Him. For example, to abide in a house means to remain in that house and to not leave it. We need a revelation to see that we are in Christ. In the New Testament there is a very small phrase of just two words, but it is the most important phrase in the universe. This phrase is "in Christ." We must have a definite seeing that we are persons who are in Christ. We must keep ourselves in Christ, remaining in Him and not going out of Him.

Question: Does the Lord put certain individuals aside for a time so that He can work again in their lives?

Answer: It is not good to analyze too much, but there is a principle that we need to see. If our intention is genuinely for the Lord and we are doing too much, the Lord will come in to stop us from our doing. God's eternal purpose is to have

Christ wrought into us, but our concept is always to do something for God. We forget that we are vessels whose purpose is not to do something but to contain something. This is the problem today. We have pointed out that many Christians simply do not care about the things of God; they love the world, having no heart for God and no desire to seek the Lord's mind or the Lord's business. There are a good number of seeking Christians, yet among them the concept of doing something for God is very strong. They do not know that they were made to be vessels and were regenerated for the purpose of containing Christ.

There is no need for us to do things for God. He can do everything. God needs us to cooperate with Him as living vessels. We need to allow God to fill us. On the day that we see this, our whole Christian concept will change, our whole being will be revolutionized, and our work and activity will be absolutely in another realm, that is, in Christ Himself. We will stop all our activity, and day by day we will say, "Lord, I am here and I am open. I am nothing but an empty vessel. I thank You that I was made in such a way to contain You. I can do nothing, Lord, yet I can contain You. Come in, fill me, and saturate my whole being with Yourself." This is the right condition and position for us to be a living Christian. If there is never a day in our whole life in which we see this, we will be pitiful and miserable persons. The sooner we see this, the better. Before he saw this, the apostle Paul was active in Judaism, in doing and in working. One day the Lord knocked him down to the ground, and he saw a heavenly vision. His whole being was stopped from doing. This is why he wrote of God revealing His Son in him, of Christ living in him, of his putting on Christ as his clothing, of Christ being formed in him, of his not being separated from Christ but keeping himself in Christ, and of Christ flowing out of him to bear the fruit of the Spirit.

This is the divine concept, and when we see this, we will be delivered from doing and working. We will realize that we are nothing but an empty vessel to contain Christ. It is not easy for the young people to see this, because young people

are very active. For the older generation it is even more difficult because too many things already occupy them.

*Question: How does a person get out of the religious "rat
race" of always going around in a circle as in a cage?*

Answer: We can escape such a situation only by revelation.
Before he was saved, Saul was very active. One day, on the
road to Damascus, the Lord met him, and he was knocked
down before the Lord. He was stopped. The revelation stops
us, and this stopping is a deliverance that rescues us from our
human effort and doing and brings us into the line of the
divine will. From that time forward, we are on the right track.

*Question: It seems that Paul was still very active after he
became a Christian. Is this not true?*

Answer: After Paul received the revelation, there is no
doubt that he acted, moved, and worked, but the motive, the
initiation, and the source were not himself but Christ. Christ
was energizing him all the time, just like a motor in a car
(Phil. 4:13). Paul's activity was an issue of his cooperation with
Christ. Seemingly, he was walking and working, but actually,
it was Christ doing these things in Paul. Twice Paul said that it
was not he but Christ. In Galatians 2:20 he said, "It is no
longer I who live, but it is Christ who lives in me," and in
1 Corinthians 15:10 he said, "I labored...yet not I but the grace
of God which is with me." The grace of God came through
Christ (John 1:17). This grace is God in Christ enjoyed and
experienced by us. It seems that Paul was saying, "It is not I,
Paul, who labor much, even more than all the other apostles;
it is God in Christ experienced by me as grace. The grace of
God works in me so that I can labor as I do." We need a revelation to see that God's intention is to work Christ into us as
our everything and to work Christ through us and out of us.
We need to be in this stream, in this line, and on this track.
All of our daily walk, living, working, service, and activity must
be an issue, an outflow, of the divine life. This is something
absolutely different from human effort.

CHAPTER FIVE

LIFE AND BUILDING
AS THE CENTRAL THOUGHT
OF THE SCRIPTURES

Although it has sixty-six books and many teachings, the entire Bible reveals to us the divine mystery. We need to find out what the central thought of this divine mystery is. Ephesians 5:32 says, "This mystery is great, but I speak with regard to Christ and the church." Christ and the church is the great mystery in the universe. Christ is the Head, and the church is the Body (Col. 1:18; Eph. 1:22-23). In order to know the central thought of this mystery, we must ask what Christ is to the church. Although it is true that Christ is the Head, the Redeemer, the Savior, the Lord, and everything to the church, the central thought is that Christ is life to the church. And what is the church to Christ? The church is the expression of Christ as life. Therefore, Christ is life to the church, and the church is the expression of Christ as life.

In the central thought of the Scriptures, Christ is revealed as life. Although Christ is revealed to us as many things, such as the Creator, the Redeemer, the Savior, and the Lord, in the central thought of the Scriptures, Christ is life to us. The Gospel of John reveals that Christ came to be life to us (10:10b). He is life (11:25; 14:6), and life is in Him (1:4). When we receive Him, we receive life. Thus, Christ as life to us is the central thought, but this is only the first part. In the Scriptures Christ is revealed, and the Body of Christ also is revealed.

Although the Body is revealed in the Scriptures, the way to practice the Body life, the church life, is rather difficult to see. After man was created, he was put in the garden of Eden in front of a tree that was called the tree of life (Gen. 2:8-9).

The tree of life signifies Christ as life to us; it is a symbol of God in Christ as life to us. Immediately after man was created, God brought up the matter of life for man's consideration. God put man before a tree, the tree of life. Moreover, beside the tree there was a river, and along the flow of the river there were gold, bdellium (a pearl-like material produced from the resin of a tree), and onyx, a precious stone (vv. 10-12). These three materials are the materials for God's building. They typify the Triune God as the basic elements of the structure of God's eternal building. Gold typifies God the Father with His divine nature, bdellium typifies Christ the Son with His redeeming and life-releasing death and His life-imparting resurrection, and precious stones typify God the Spirit with His transforming and building work. At the beginning of the Scriptures there is a picture that includes the tree of life with a river and three precious materials, and at the end of the Scriptures there is another picture, the picture of the New Jerusalem (Rev. 21:2—22:5), a city in which the tree of life grows and the river of water of life flows, and which is built with three precious materials—gold, pearls, and precious stones. Thus, the pictures at the two ends of the Scriptures correspond with each other; both pictures portray life and building.

Building is a crucial matter in the Scriptures. Christ is life, and the church is a building. The first time the Scriptures mention the church, it is related to the matter of building. Matthew 16:18 says, "I also say to you that you are Peter, and upon this rock I will build My church, and the gates of Hades shall not prevail against it." In this verse the church is clearly portrayed as a building. Life and building are the central thought of the Scriptures. In the first picture in the Scriptures, in Genesis 2, there is the tree of life with a flowing river. The issue of the flow of the river is three kinds of materials for building. In the last picture, at the end of the Scriptures, there is a city built with three kinds of materials. In this city are the tree of life and the river of water of life. Hence, from the beginning of the Scriptures to the end, the central thought is life and building. It is more accurate to say that the central thought is life for building. Life is Christ, the building is the church, and Christ as life is for the church as the building. We must be very clear that the central thought of the Scriptures is Christ coming to us to be enjoyed and experienced as life for the purpose of producing a building. This building is Christ's Body, the church, which is Christ's expression.

The pictures at the beginning and the end of the Scriptures may be likened to the beginning and end of an architectural plan. The picture at the beginning of the Bible is like an architectural drawing, a blueprint, that shows the intended building. The picture at the end of the Bible is like a photograph of the finished building. In the entire universe God has a plan to build a divine building. The Bible is a definition of God's plan. In Genesis 2 there is an architectural drawing, a blueprint, and in Revelation 21 and 22 there is a photograph, a picture, of the completed building.

The picture in Genesis 2 includes created man, but at that time created man was separate from the tree of life, the river, the gold, the bdellium, and the onyx stone. He was merely in front of these items. He only saw these things, but he had nothing to do with them intrinsically. God's intention, however, was that all these items would be wrought into man. In God's intention the tree of life had to enter into man to be man's life, and the river had to flow in man and out of man. Furthermore, man, who was created of dust (v. 7), had to be transformed into precious stone. The Lord Jesus confirmed God's intention when He changed Peter's name from Simon to Peter, which means "a stone" (Matt. 16:18; John 1:42). Later, Peter wrote that the believers in Christ are living stones who are being built up into a spiritual house (1 Pet. 2:5).

To change a man of clay into a precious stone requires regeneration (John 3:6; 1 Pet. 1:3, 23) and transformation (Rom. 12:2; 2 Cor. 3:18). Our being transformed from clay into precious stone begins with the regeneration of our spirit. At the time we are regenerated, there is a small piece of precious stone in our spirit, but around this piece of stone there is a great deal of clay. All the clay must be changed into precious stone through the process of transformation.

In 1 Corinthians 3 the apostle Paul told us that he was a master builder who laid the foundation, which is Christ, for

God's building, and another builds upon this foundation with gold, silver, and precious stones (vv. 10-12a). In verse 12 silver, signifying Christ's redemption, is referred to instead of bdellium (Gen. 2:12) and pearl (Rev. 21:21a) because of man's need of redemption after the fall. In the New Testament the building work is carried out by the Triune God as gold, pearls, and precious stones being wrought into the believers. At the end of the New Testament and of the entire Scriptures, there is a city built up with three kinds of precious material—gold, pearls, and precious stones. Furthermore, the tree of life is growing in this city, and the river of water of life is flowing in it. At this point the tree of life, the river of water of life, and the precious materials have been wrought into and mingled with man. In the final picture, the picture of the New Jerusalem, the tree of life and the flowing river are within man, and man has become precious materials for God's building. Thus, in the New Jerusalem we can see both life and building.

CHRIST BEING LIFE FOR GOD'S BUILDING

If we keep the pictures at the two ends of the Scriptures before us as we read the Scriptures, we will see that the entire Scriptures deal with nothing but Christ as life for God's building. Christ is life for the purpose of producing the materials that will be built up as a spiritual building, a spiritual house. This spiritual house is the Body of Christ as a dwelling place to God and a bride to Christ. In the picture in Genesis 2 we see the tree of life, the flow of the river, the materials for the building, and a woman, Eve, built by God to be a bride for Adam (vv. 21-24). Adam is a type of Christ (Rom. 5:14), and Eve is a type of the church (Eph. 5:31-32). In the picture in Revelation 21 and 22 we again see the tree of life, the flow of the river, and a woman built with the same three kinds of precious materials. This woman, the New Jerusalem, is the wife of the Lamb (21:9-10).

The central thought of the Scriptures is that we must receive Christ as life and experience Christ as life so that we will first be regenerated, then transformed to be the precious materials for the building, and then built up together (Eph. 2:22; 4:12, 16; 1 Pet. 2:5). The ultimate issue of such a process is a building, the holy city, New Jerusalem, which is the tabernacle of God and the wife of the Lamb (Rev. 21:2-3, 9-10). Once we know the central thought of the Scriptures, we must be responsible for two things. First, we must accept, receive, experience, and apply Christ as our life, and second, we must be transformed. After we have been regenerated, we must be transformed into precious materials. We were created of clay, and we must be transformed into stones. Then we must be transformed further from stones into precious stones and be built up together as a building. This building is the church. In other words, the central thought of the Scriptures is that Christ is life to us to regenerate us and transform us into precious materials for His building. We must be responsible to receive Christ, apply Christ, and appropriate Christ to ourselves as life that we may be regenerated, transformed into precious materials, and built up together with others as the Body of Christ, which is God's dwelling place and Christ's bride. If we see such a vision, it will change our concept radically. This vision will revolutionize our entire being and conduct. We will know where we are and what we must do.

By seeing this vision, we will also be qualified, equipped, and in the right position to see and apprehend all the spiritual things in a proper way. The Scriptures and all the spiritual things are like a jigsaw puzzle. If we intend to put a jigsaw puzzle together, we must first see the picture. With the picture in our mind, we can put all the pieces of the puzzle together correctly. Today as they read the Scriptures, many Christians do not have the picture. They put the "head" where the "tail" should be, or they put the "tail" on the "head." The result is a monster. Often as I was listening to people expound the Scriptures, I said to myself, "Dear friend, you are making the church a monster. It is obvious that you have not seen the picture." First, we must see the pictures in Genesis 1 and 2 and Revelation 21 and 22. If we have these two pictures, we will know the central thought of the Scriptures and will be able to put every piece of the jigsaw puzzle into the right place to eventually form the full picture. We will know where we are and what we need to do. This vision will direct our whole conduct and control our whole thought. The vision is to receive Christ as life that we may be regenerated, transformed, and built up with others. Life and building, or life for building, is the central thought of the Scriptures. We are transformed by contacting Christ, receiving Christ, and applying Christ again and again. This is the proper meaning of the Lord's table, which is unto the remembrance of the Lord. As a young Christian who was newly saved, I thought that to remember the Lord was to remember how great, glorious, kind, and gracious the Lord is. Later, I received the light to know the proper meaning of the remembrance of the Lord. When the Lord instituted the table with His disciples, He said, "This is My body which is being given for you; do this in remembrance of Me" (Luke 22:19). The real meaning of the remembrance of the Lord is to receive the Lord by eating Him. To remember the Lord in a proper way, we need to receive something of the Lord into our being. Therefore, whenever we come to the Lord's table to break the bread and drink the cup, we need to receive the Lord once more by exercising our spirit. The remembrance of the Lord is not merely a human remembrance by using our mind to consider and remember what the Lord is to us. The proper meaning of remembering the Lord is to receive the Lord once again. Whenever we come to the Lord's table, we must exercise our spirit to receive something of the Lord. The Lord's table is a testimony, testifying that we live by the Lord (John 6:57). Day by day, morning and evening, and moment by moment we live by taking Christ as our life. This is our way of living. On the Lord's Day, the first day of the week, we come together to testify this to the universe, especially to the rulers and authorities in the heavenly places.

The Christian life is a life of taking Christ as everything. By such a life we are gradually transformed, and our nature is changed from clay into stone and from stone into precious stone. Then we are built up together with others as a spiritual building. This is the central thought of the Scriptures, and this will check us, direct us, and control us in our doing, our living, and our work.

QUESTIONS AND ANSWERS

Question: Can you tell us more about the process of transformation?

Answer: Precious stones are not created directly but are formed through the transforming of created materials. For example, a diamond is formed from carbon, a created substance, that is put into an environment of intense heat and high pressure for a period of time. We were originally created of clay, but one day the Lord put Himself into us as a new element in order that we may experience a metabolic change. This metabolic change needs not only the Lord as the new element to replace our old element, but also an environment of heat and pressure. Many times the Lord puts us into an environment of heat and pressure. We need a certain amount of burning and pressing; otherwise, we will remain created material that has not been transformed. In order to be transformed from clay into precious stones for God's building, we must pass through a process of burning and pressing. We need not be afraid of this, but when we experience it, we should know where we are.

Question: I have realized that Christ is my life and that He is transforming me into a precious stone through trials and tribulations to conform me more and more to be like Him. But as far as the matter of building is concerned, this is something new. Can you say something more about building?

Answer: Most Christians think that they must be spiritual, not realizing that eventually they need to be built up with other Christians. To be genuinely spiritual means to be transformed into a precious stone in order to be built up with others. However, today many Christians merely seek a certain kind of spirituality and do not know anything about being built up. They can be likened to beautiful stones that are exhibited in a museum for others' appreciation. The purpose of our being transformed is not to be an exhibit. We are transformed to be the materials for God's building. Individual spirituality does not count for anything. We need to be spiritual in order to be built up with others. Without being tested by the building, we might think that we are spiritual, but when we are put into the building, we are examined as to whether our spirituality is genuine or not. A young brother who is a bachelor and is not related to anyone may dream that he is more spiritual than Martin Luther, but once he has a wife and three or four children, and once he begins to serve together with other brothers in the church life, he will be tested. Then he will know where he is and what he is. He will find that he is a most unspiritual person and that whatever spirituality he thinks he has is false and is simply in his imagination. We need to be built up with others. If we can be spiritual with our wife, with our children, and with the brothers, our spirituality is genuine. We need to be spiritual and to be built up as well. The more individualistic we are, the more it is proven that we are not spiritual.

In the Far East there are a few single sisters who think that they are very spiritual. I knew a single sister who was very nice, who loved the Lord, and who sought the Lord. Everyone admired her and considered her better than an angel. After she married, several times she came to me in tears concerning her husband. Later, she had children. As the children grew up, there were many problems. The husband and the children were all trials to her. After learning all the lessons, she testified, "Dear brothers and sisters, before I was married, my spirituality was absolutely false. Today, after the Lord put me through fire with a husband and children, I can say that there might be something in my spirituality that is really of the Lord."

Many Christians today remain in the old condition without any transformation. Because of this, there is an urgent need for messages like this one to render help to the Lord's children. After receiving this kind of help, we will realize the genuine church life, which is not merely to come together but to experience Christ more and more. Christ is life to us, and we, the church, the Body of Christ, are the expression of Christ. God planned in eternity past and has been seeking in generation after generation to be life to man in His Son, the Lord Jesus Christ, that His redeemed and regenerated ones may be transformed and built up together as a corporate expression of Christ.

Question: Is it not true that before the Lord's coming, it will be impossible for the church as a whole to actually be His Body?

Answer: In the Scriptures, especially related to the matter of the church, there is the principle of the overcomers, the remnant. As a whole, the church has failed the Lord, but today, before His coming back, the Lord is calling the overcomers. This is revealed in the seven epistles to the seven churches in Revelation 2 and 3. There the Lord spoke many things concerning the churches, and at the end of each epistle He issued a call for the overcomers, the remnant. On the one hand, we must expect that all the Lord's children will be helped in a general way, but on the other hand, we must realize that, according to the prophetic teaching of the Scriptures, before the Lord's coming back only a comparatively small number of believers will respond to the Lord's calling and become the overcomers to fill the place that the church as a whole has lost. As a whole the church has failed the Lord, but part of the church will answer the Lord's call to be the overcomers to fulfill God's purpose on behalf of the whole church. This is the principle of the overcomers, the principle of the remnant.

In Revelation the New Jerusalem is the wife of the Lamb, Christ. In chapter 12 there is a universal woman who is about to give birth to a man-child (vv. 1-2). The woman symbolizes the totality of God's people on earth, and the man-child is the stronger part of God's people. In biblical typology, a male signifies a strong one, and a female, a weaker one (1 Pet. 3:7). The majority of the church, signified by the woman, is weak, and only a small part, signified by the man-child, is strong. This stronger part will shepherd the nations with an iron rod (Rev. 12:5). According to Revelation 2:26-27, those who will shepherd the nations with an iron rod are the overcomers. Thus, the man-child is composed of the overcomers, the stronger part of the Body of Christ. In the eyes of God the whole Body, the whole church, is like a woman, a weaker vessel.

We realize that there is an urgent need because there are many seeking ones in different localities. Although they may not know what they hunger for, we know that they hunger for Christ as life and for the real expression of the church. The

Holy Spirit works this hunger into the spirit of the seeking saints. Within the seeking saints is a deep sense which nothing can satisfy. Revivals will not satisfy their hunger, for the more revivals there are, the more hunger they feel. Christ is the satisfying life to be experienced by all His seeking ones. Once they discover the secret of experiencing Christ, they will be satisfied. They are also seeking for a genuine church life, without which they will never be satisfied. This is because they need a family, a home. Life is Christ, and the home, the family, is the church. We must minister Christ as life to these hungry, seeking saints and afford them a spiritual home, that is, the church.

A TESTIMONY OF THE LORD'S LEADING

Two and a half years ago I came to this country for the second time. I went to New York and stayed with the church in New York City from the fall of 1960 until the end of the year, a period of two and a half months. In December I came back to the West en route to the Far East. At that time I had a deep and clear sense that the Lord would do something in this country, especially along the West Coast.

I told the brother with whom I was staying my feeling, but he would not believe me and thought that I was dreaming. Even I must admit that I had no intention of coming to America a third time. Yet I was brought, and even forced, by the Lord to come here a third time, and my visit lasted for a whole year. At the end of October, as I tried to leave, the Lord put His hand upon me to keep me here. The Lord closed the door on whatever way I tried to leave. I had prepared everything for my return to the Far East, but the Lord did everything to frustrate me, and I had to submit myself to Him. I told Him, "Even though there is a large work in the Far East, if You want me to stay here, I must go along with You." At that time I was staying in Seattle. I called a brother in San Francisco, and he was astonished to learn that I was still in America. I asked him to go to Sacramento with me. Then I called a brother in Los Angeles, and he too was astonished, thinking that I had gone back to the Far East already. I told the brothers that I would go to San Francisco, then to Sacramento, and after that to Los Angeles in order to stay there for a longer time. That was the end of November. Consider what has happened since then. In one place the number coming together has increased from six persons to about seventy. Something has happened in Los Angeles, and many things have happened along the West Coast in different cities. Wherever I go, I meet seeking ones who tell me that it is only in the last two or three years that something has happened among them. People tell me the same thing, that is, that if I had come earlier than this, no one would have listened to me. It is only within these two or three years that something has happened. Now after hearing us, they feel that what we minister to them is exactly what they need.

Chapter Six

THE CHURCH AS THE INCREASE OF CHRIST

John 3:6 says, "That which is born of the Spirit is spirit." According to this verse, the real meaning of regeneration is to be born of the Holy Spirit in our human spirit. Verse 29 of the same chapter says, "He who has the bride is the bridegroom." Christ is the Bridegroom, the One who has the bride, and the bride is the church of Christ. Then verse 30 says, "He must increase." He, that is, Christ the Son of God, must increase. In verse 29 we have the bride, and in verse 30 we have the increase. This indicates that the bride of Christ is the increase of Christ. In John 3, therefore, we see the bride, the increase, and the regenerated spirit. If we read this chapter carefully, we will realize that all the reborn, regenerated, believers composed together are the increase of Christ to be a bride, a counterpart, to match Him. The new birth, the bride, and the increase are three main items in this chapter. By the new birth Christ is increased, and this increase is a corporate bride who will marry Christ as His counterpart to match Him.

In John 12:24 the Lord Jesus said, "Truly, truly, I say to you, Unless the grain of wheat falls into the ground and dies, it abides alone; but if it dies, it bears much fruit." In this verse *much fruit* refers to the many grains of wheat borne as fruit by the one grain of wheat. One grain of wheat falls to the earth and dies, and when it grows up, it bears many grains. Originally, it was one grain, but after it dies and is resurrected, it becomes many grains. The one original grain is the Lord Jesus Himself, and the many grains are we, the Lord's believers, who are the increase of the one grain. After dying and resurrecting, one grain becomes many grains. Thus, the one grain has been increased. The many grains are the increase of the original grain.

Ephesians 2:15 says, "That He might create the two in Himself into one new man." *The two* refers to the Jewish believers and the Gentile believers. Christ created the Jews and the Gentiles in Himself into one new man. The next verse tells us what the one new man is: "And might reconcile both [the Jews and the Gentiles] in one Body to God through the cross" (v. 16a). According to this verse the one new man is the one Body, the church. Many Christians have a wrong concept, thinking that the new man here is not one but many. However, there is only one new man in the whole universe, and this new man is not an individual man but a corporate man composed of all the believers together as one. Because this one new man is the Body of Christ, the church, each believer is only a part, a member, of the unique new man. Thus, according to this passage the church, which is the Body of Christ, is a new man.

Ephesians 4:22-24 says, "Put off...the old man...and...be renewed in the spirit of your mind and put on the new man." If we remember what the new man in chapter 2 is, we can understand the right meaning of putting on the new man in these verses. Since the new man is the Body, the church, to put on the new man is to put on the Body of Christ, to put on the church as our living, to practice the church life. To put on the new man is not merely to put on something new of Christ. If we read the book of Ephesians carefully from chapter 1 through chapter 4, we will know that to put on the new man simply means to put on the Body of Christ, to put on the church as our living.

In order to have the church life, that is, to put on the Body of Christ, the new man, we need to put off the old man. The secret to putting off the old man and putting on the new man is to be renewed in the spirit of our mind. How much we put off the old man and put on the new man depends on how much we have been transformed by being renewed in the spirit of our mind (Rom. 12:2).

Colossians 3:9b-11 says, "You have put off the old man...and have put on the new man,...where there cannot be Greek and

Jew, circumcision and uncircumcision, barbarian, Scythian, slave, free man, but Christ is all and in all." In the new man there is nothing but Christ. There is no Greek or Jew, no circumcision or uncircumcision, no barbarian, Scythian, slave, or free man, but Christ is all and in all. Therefore, strictly speaking, the new man is Christ Himself. The Body of Christ, the church, is Christ Himself. This corresponds with 1 Corinthians 12:12, which says, "For even as the body is one and has many members, yet all the members of the body, being many, are one body, so also is the Christ." This verse, using the human body to typify the mystical Body of Christ, indicates that Christ is the Body.

THE REALITY OF THE CHURCH

In the previous chapter we covered the first aspect of the realization of the eternal purpose of God. To realize the eternal purpose of God, we need to know Christ as our life. God's eternal purpose is to work Christ into us, to have Christ wrought into us, and to make Christ life to us. The first aspect is for the second aspect. If we experience Christ as life, automatically we will have the church life; we will realize the life of the Body of Christ, the church. The more we experience Christ as life, the more we will desire to be related with other believers. If we love the world or live in sin, we will have no desire to see the believers or fellowship with the brothers and sisters. But the more we live by Christ, take Christ as our life, and experience Christ as life, the more we will desire to have fellowship with the brothers and sisters and to be related with other Christians. Therefore, the more we take Christ as our life, the more we will have the church life.

The church is not an organization. The church is the realization of Christ as life to us. If you do not live in Christ, and if I do not take Christ as my life, we may come together to form a church based on certain conditions and terms, and we may hold a conference to elect some leaders. However, the result will not be a church but a human, religious organization. A genuine church is Christ Himself realized and experienced by His believers. The more we experience Christ, the more we long to be related to others, and the more we live by Christ, the more we desire to be built up together with others. If everyone lives by Christ, there will be a common desire to be related to one another. We will come together in the name of the Lord and in the Lord Himself to have Christ as our center and as everything to us. Then we will have a new church as the realization of Christ. This church will be Christ Himself mingled with a group of believers as one. It will be an organism constituted of Christ and those who experience Christ as their life. In this way the church will be just Christ Himself.

The church comes into being by regeneration. One day the Holy Spirit entered into us, bringing Christ into us to regenerate us. This means that Christ was born once more, in us. Whenever a sinner receives Christ as his Savior, the Holy Spirit brings Christ into this person to be born once more, in him. In regeneration, not only are we born again, but Christ also is born once more, within us. From that day forward there is something of Christ in us. Hence, there is something of Christ in every regenerated person. This is sufficient for the new birth, for regeneration, but it is not sufficient for the church to come into existence. To have the church in reality, every regenerated one must deny himself, reject the old man, and live out Christ, allowing Christ to be expressed through him. Then the reality of the church will come into being.

Therefore, the church is Christ born within us and expressed through us. If Christ were to come down from heaven and stand among us, this Christ would not be the church. Only the Christ who enters into us and is born in us to be our life, only the Christ who lives Himself out and expresses Himself through us—only this Christ is the reality of the church. The church is Christ born into us and lived out and expressed through us.

THE CHURCH BEING CHRIST'S INCREASE

The church is the increase of Christ. It is the bride who will marry Christ as His counterpart to match Him. God created Adam as a bachelor (Gen. 2:18). After a certain time, God caused him to sleep and took a rib from his side, and He built that rib into a woman who could be Adam's bride to match him (vv. 21-23). Thus, the woman who was Adam's bride was

Adam's increase. Adam was no longer a bachelor, but he and his bride became a couple. Eve was Adam's increase, and this increase was a part of Adam, something that had come out of Adam. Adam is a type of Christ (Rom. 5:14), and Eve is a type of the church, which comes out of Christ (Eph. 5:31-32). Without the church, we may say that Christ is single, a "bachelor" without an increase. One day God put Christ to sleep on the cross, and He opened His side and took something out of Him (John 19:34). Both Adam's rib and the water that flowed out of Christ's side on the cross are types of the resurrection life of Christ, which cannot be broken or destroyed. When Christ was crucified, none of His bones was broken (v. 36). This indicates that Christ's resurrection life is unbreakable and indestructible. The resurrection life of Christ that flowed out of Him on the cross becomes the Body of Christ, the church. Thus, the church is something out of Christ Himself and is the increase of Christ. When the Holy Spirit enters into us to regenerate our spirit, the resurrection life of Christ enters into us. At that very moment there is something of Christ in us. When the resurrection life of Christ is lived out and expressed through us, there is the reality of the church, the increase of Christ to match Him as His counterpart. The church is the increase of Christ and the bride of Christ.

PUTTING ON THE NEW MAN
FOR THE REALITY OF THE CHURCH

We have pointed out that the church is the resurrected Christ as life being born into us, lived out from within us, and expressed through us. This Christ is the church, and this church is the counterpart, the increase, and the bride of Christ. In order to realize the genuine church life, we need to put off the old man, which is our self, our soulish life, by rejecting our mind, emotion, and will, and we need to put on the new man, which is Christ with the church and the church with Christ. To put on Christ with the church and to put on the church with Christ requires us to be renewed in the spirit of our mind. Originally, our regenerated spirit is not the spirit of our mind. However, when we reject our self and deny the old life, this spirit expands into our mind and becomes the spirit of our mind. The element of the spirit spreads into our mind and renews it with a new concept. By such a spirit we are delivered from our old mind, our old concepts, and our mind becomes a new mind, a renewed mind, with a new concept. The church life depends on our putting off the old man and putting on the new man, having our mind renewed by the spirit. To be renewed in the spirit of our mind means that all our old concepts must be given up, and we must have an absolutely new concept; that is, we must have the mind of the Holy Spirit, the mind of Christ (1 Cor. 2:16), a mind that is filled with our regenerated human spirit, which is mingled with the Holy Spirit (6:17), and is under the control of our spirit. By such a renewing, we put off the old man and put on the new man. This ushers us into the reality of the church life.

To apply this renewing, we may use the example of a brother who is clever at making money. He is reborn, regenerated, and he has the Holy Spirit within him, yet he still lives by the old man. Therefore, there is no possibility for him to have the church life. He may sometimes come to the church meetings and may also fellowship with the brothers, but whoever meets him has the sense that he is only a brother who is good at making money. After some time, certain brothers who are with him may become exactly the same as he is—good moneymakers. With such brothers there is no reality of the church life. However, one day this brother may have a turn to the Lord. He may realize that to be a Christian is not to live by the old man but to live by the new man, that is, by the regenerated spirit. Then he may learn how to reject his old man and how to live by the new man. As a result, whenever he comes to the church meetings and whenever we meet him, we sense that there is something of Christ in him. Because he is such a person, we desire to be related to him and to be one with him. Since this brother and we are in the same condition, with all of us there is the reality of the church life, because the reality of the church life is Christ Himself realized by us. We have the reality of the church life and are in the Body life because our entire concept has been transformed. The old thought, the old concept, and the old way of thinking are gone, and there is something new in our thinking. Our view of things is very different from what it was before. Thus, there is the reality of the church life because Christ is realized and experienced by us.

BEING BLENDED TOGETHER AS ONE

We are also the many grains of Christ. In order for many grains to become one loaf, the grains must be crushed and blended into flour. The church life requires us to be "crushed" so that we can be blended with others to become one loaf. We are many, yet we are one body, one bread (1 Cor. 10:17). Originally we were many grains, but now we are one bread. It is easy to speak of the church, but the church requires us to die, to be crushed and broken, and to lose our individuality. If we remain individual grains, we will always compare ourselves with others and be aware of the differences between ourselves and others. However, after a number of grains have been crushed and ground into flour, there is no longer any possibility of discerning which is which. All have become flour to be blended together and made into dough, which is then put in an oven and baked to become one loaf. The church life is Christ expressed through us as we are blended together as one. This oneness is the church life, the realization of the Body of Christ.

PAYING THE PRICE FOR THE CHURCH LIFE

You may say that to be crushed and ground is too high a price. In buying anything, if you try to save money, you may suffer a great loss. You may pay five dollars for a piece of clothing and end up with something worth fifty cents. An article of clothing that costs fifty dollars may seem to you to be too expensive, but a person who knows clothing well may consider it very inexpensive. By paying fifty dollars, such a person may get a piece of clothing worth five hundred dollars. He paid more than you did, but he got more than he paid for. If we would pay the price to realize the genuine church life, we could never imagine what kind of gain we will have. The church life is an unsearchable, immeasurable gain.

If all the believers would pay the price to realize the church life, the whole world would be turned upside down.

There were only one hundred twenty on the day of Pentecost, but consider the impact that they had. It is not a loss to pay the price to have the church life; on the contrary, it is a great gain. It is worth investing our whole life, even risking our whole life, for the gaining of the church life. The Lord today is looking for a group of people who will pay the price to realize the church life.

QUESTIONS AND ANSWERS

Question: Do you believe that a division exists between those who deny the self and those who do not?

Answer: Actually, the more we deny our self, the more we will be related with others, not only with those who deny themselves but also with those who do not deny themselves. Instead of separating ourselves from those who do not deny themselves, we will be sympathetic toward them. Division is due to different denominations, sects, and organizations. We must give up organization, denominations, and sects, but we must not give up the dear saints.

Question: In that case, do you feel one cannot experience a normal church life within a denomination?

Answer: It is impossible to have a normal church life in a denomination. Although I love all the Lord's children, I must be honest with them before God. The matter of denominations is the most sinful thing. How much damage has been done to the Lord's Body by denominations! Nevertheless, my ministry is to minister Christ to people, to help them to know Christ and to realize the genuine church life. If we love the Lord and take Him as our life, experiencing Him day by day, we will be outside the denominations.

Question: Should our children continue to attend a denomination in order to be taught the Bible?

Answer: The Lord's children need to learn one thing, that is, to consider the Lord's will and nothing else. We must do the Lord's will regardless of everything. We should be assured that if we do the Lord's will, the Lord will bless us and take care of our children. Sooner or later we will see the Lord bless our family. Our only consideration must be the will of the

Lord, and we must be bold to act according to this will. Everything else will be taken care of by the Lord.

Question: In the past many have taken a similar stand to yours and called people out of the denominational way, but then they fell into the same error of sectarianism or denominationalism. How can we preserve ourselves from this?

Answer: In the past centuries quite a number of the Lord's saints called people out of denominations. However, I am not calling people to leave the denominations; I am ministering Christ to them. When we live by Christ, something will happen. It is an empty thing simply to call people to leave denominations, and it does not work. Instead, we should minister Christ to people and help them to experience Him day by day. Christ will energize and strengthen them to go on, and they will be filled with Him. If they experience Christ in a practical way, they will certainly give up denominations. Yet for them to give up denominations is merely a small thing on the negative side. It is a much greater matter for them to live Christ that Christ may be expressed. We must pay our full attention to this positive aspect.

Question: If, as a group, we are experiencing the Body of Christ, what should our attitude and relationship be to other true, regenerated believers, who are our brothers even though they do not experience the Body?

Answer: Concerning all genuine, regenerated believers, we must be absolutely open to them. We should never think that we are different from them. They are the Lord's children, and we are also; we are believers, and they are as well. Therefore, we should be open to them and endeavor to fellowship with them. If possible, we should help them and also receive help from them.

Today what we emphasize is not leaving the denominations but experiencing Christ. My attitude is not to pay attention to the matter of denominations but simply to minister Christ to others. As long as we experience Christ, the Christ whom we experience will do many things within us. This is something positive. Merely to leave the denominations and attempt to practice the Body life is empty, and it is not what we are seeking today. If we are not seeking and experiencing Christ as our life, and if it is not Christ in us who energizes us and makes us clear concerning God's will, we should not leave our denomination. Actually, it is better to remain there. We must allow Christ to bring us out of all the hindrances and things that are foreign to the Body of Christ.

Furthermore, even our talk about the Holy Spirit may be unrelated to Christ. The Pentecostal movement began in England in the middle of the nineteenth century. When those in the Pentecostal movement speak of the Holy Spirit, it is not related to the experience of Christ in daily life. Thirty years ago in China there were five different branches of the Pentecostal movement: the Assembly of God, the Apostolic Faith, the Jesus Home, the True Jesus Church, and the Spiritual Grace movement. The Spiritual Grace movement was the most prevailing, and in a short time it swept through all of northern China, including my hometown and province. Day after day they spoke of the manifestation of the Holy Spirit and speaking in tongues, but they simply did not know how to experience Christ as their life. Hence, this movement did not last long. We certainly do not oppose the Holy Spirit; indeed, we need the Holy Spirit. But we need to realize that the genuine experience of the Holy Spirit is for glorifying Christ. The Holy Spirit is the Spirit of Christ (Rom. 8:9); not only so, the Lord Jesus said that when the Holy Spirit came, He would not speak from Himself but would glorify Christ (John 16:13-15). Today there is too much talk about the Holy Spirit and very little experience of Christ. I discovered the shortcomings of these Pentecostal groups by attending their meetings and spending many days with them. Apparently, in their meetings they were powerful, but as soon as they went home, the husbands lost their temper with their wives. When they prayed, "Hallelujah! Thank You, Jesus. Hallelujah!" it seemed that the Holy Spirit was with them, but the reality of Christ as life was missing. Thus, I doubted whether in fact it was the Holy Spirit whom they were experiencing.

The problem is this: If we experience something of the Holy Spirit but do not go further to apprehend and experience Christ as our life, there will be an opening for the enemy to do things to damage the Lord's work. Recently an Episcopal priest brought a certain revival into the Episcopalian church by helping people to experience the Holy Spirit and speak in tongues. However, later someone in the inner circle of that movement admitted that they needed something more. The so-called experience of the Holy Spirit is just a beginning and should lead us to Christ. One brother has compared the situation among the Pentecostals to the time when Abraham sent his servant to find a wife for his son Isaac. The servant gave Rebecca many gifts for the purpose of leading Rebecca to Isaac so that she might be married to him. Regrettably, today's "Rebecca" is satisfied just to have the gifts. A gift should bring people to its giver. Like Rebecca, we should not value the gift but should treasure our Husband, Christ. However, most Pentecostal believers are satisfied with gifts such as speaking in tongues and divine healing. They "play" with the gifts and forget the Giver. I observed and studied all these things. Not one of the five Pentecostal groups in China lasted very long, and I did not see anyone among them grow deeper in his spiritual life.

In fact, from its beginning in 1927 the Spiritual Grace movement lasted only ten years. During that time it swept through the whole of northern China. Not only was it short-lived; it also caused much damage to the preaching of the gospel because those in that movement went to extremes. Some of them, under the influence of being "full of the Holy Spirit," left their families, homes, wives, and children in order to go to distant places to preach the gospel. Because they felt that they were filled with the Holy Spirit, they did peculiar and even shameful things in their meetings. There were some who were called "holy jumpers" and others who were called "holy rollers." We need to be impressed that the Holy Spirit is the One who bears witness to the Lord Jesus, who declares Christ to us, and who makes Christ real to us as our life. Whenever we experience the Holy Spirit, we need to turn ourselves to Christ. The more we experience Christ, the safer it is. Our urgent need today is to know and experience Christ and then to have the genuine church life. We need to be very general and not hold on to anything special. We must also be moderate and not practice anything that is extreme. With the

Pentecostal experiences, some part is genuinely of the Holy Spirit, but a great part is of human emotion. After Pentecostal believers receive the experience of the Holy Spirit, they become emotional. Hence, their experience is a manifestation not of divine power but of human emotion. They mix emotional things together with spiritual things. In contrast, we need to be very moderate and general, and we need to learn to apply the cross to our old man. Then we will be saved from an emotional atmosphere, and we will be preserved in the genuine experience of Christ.

Chapter Seven

BEING IN THE SPIRIT

In this chapter we will consider the matter of being in the spirit. In order to see this matter, first we need to realize that the Bible reveals that there are two spirits: the divine Spirit, that is, God Himself, and the human spirit, that is, our spirit. John 4:24 says, "God is Spirit, and those who worship Him must worship in spirit and truthfulness." We must realize that the God whom we serve, the God in whom we believe and whom we worship, is a Spirit. Whenever we intend to contact something, we must know its nature in order to know the right way to contact it. We may worship and serve God, but many of us simply do not realize that the God whom we worship and serve is a Spirit. We must realize that the nature, substance, and character of God is Spirit. If we realize that God is Spirit, we will know the right way to contact and worship God. John 4:24 also speaks of the human spirit. A spirit can be contacted only by a spirit. Since God is Spirit, if we desire to contact God, the divine Spirit, we must contact Him in and with our spirit. It is certainly not possible to contact God by means of our mind or our body. God is Spirit, and therefore we need to worship God by means of our spirit.

The matter of worship includes all the kinds of contact we can have with God. To worship God does not mean simply to bow down to Him. Rather, it means to contact God in different ways, including to pray to God, to praise God, to trust in God, to have fellowship with God, and to speak for God. Worship is an all-inclusive matter that covers every phase of our contact with God.

Whatever we do to contact God must be in our spirit and with our spirit, because God is Spirit. We cannot contact God by any other means. This is a fixed principle, something spoken by the Lord. The Lord clearly tells us in John 4:24 that God is Spirit and that to worship God, to contact God, we must be in spirit. This principle can never be broken; there are no exceptions. In the matter of worshipping God there are two spirits: the divine Spirit and the human spirit.

THE REGENERATED SPIRIT

Another verse that refers to the two spirits is John 3:6, which says, "That which is born of the flesh is flesh, and that which is born of the Spirit is spirit." There is a comparison here between the flesh and the spirit. Flesh is born of the flesh, and spirit is born of the Spirit. In this verse the first spirit mentioned is the Spirit of God, and the second spirit is our spirit, which is born of the Spirit. This second spirit is not simply our original spirit created by God; rather, it is our original spirit that has been regenerated, that is, reborn, born again, of the Spirit of God. Rebirth, regeneration, takes place when our human spirit is born of and by the Holy Spirit. Through such a rebirth the Lord Jesus as life is imparted into us. The Holy Spirit of God enters into our spirit to enliven our dead spirit and also to bring the Lord Jesus as life into our spirit. Hence, our spirit is not only enlivened but also born with Christ as life by the Holy Spirit.

Soon after I was saved, I endeavored to find a book that would give me a proper definition of regeneration. I also asked certain pastors and Bible teachers to define this matter for me, but their answers failed to satisfy me. One day, however, the Lord revealed to me what rebirth, or regeneration, is. Regeneration involves the Spirit of God coming into our dead spirit to enliven it. However, the word *enliven* does not adequately express the meaning of regeneration. Regeneration means that the Holy Spirit comes into us to impart life to us, to give us life, and to make us alive. He does this by bringing Christ as life into us and imparting Christ into us. As a result, our dead spirit is not only made alive; it is also born.

There is a difference between being made alive and being born. For example, the Lord's raising up Lazarus was merely an enlivening, not a birth. But when the Holy Spirit comes into us and enlivens our spirit, He makes our spirit alive and also imparts the Lord Jesus as life into us. This is not merely an enlivening but a birth as well, an enlivening with a birth. To be enlivened means to be made alive; this does not necessarily involve the adding of another element. In contrast, regeneration involves the adding into us of something that we did not have originally. When the Holy Spirit comes into us to enliven our spirit, He adds Christ Himself into our spirit. Now in our regenerated spirit there is the divine life, which is Christ Himself (John 11:25; 14:6; Rom. 8:10). This makes our spirit not merely an enlivened spirit but a regenerated spirit.

Today many Christians realize only that their dead spirit has been made alive by the Holy Spirit. They have no idea that in their spirit something has been added, which is Christ Himself as life. Now our spirit is not only an enlivened spirit but also a spirit that is regenerated with Christ as life. We have such a reborn spirit, a regenerated spirit. This is the significance of our rebirth.

We have pointed out that regeneration is the enlivening of our spirit by the Holy Spirit with the imparting of Christ as life into us. Through regeneration we receive a second life, a life in addition to our original human life. Originally we had only the human life from our parents, but now we have the divine life from God. This second life is God Himself in Christ, and this life is in our regenerated spirit. Therefore, God is Spirit, and we have a spirit that has been regenerated with Christ as life by the Holy Spirit.

THE SPIRIT OF GOD WITNESSING WITH OUR SPIRIT

A third verse that speaks of the two spirits is Romans 8:16. This verse says, "The Spirit Himself witnesses with our spirit that we are children of God." According to this verse we know that we are children of God because there is an inner witness within us. This inner witness is the Holy Spirit within us, who bears witness with our spirit. In the past when someone asked me, "Brother Lee, how do I know that I am a child of God?" I told him, "Just say, 'I am not a child of God.'" The person would invariably answer, "I cannot say this." When I asked him why, he would tell me that he had no peace to say this. I would go on to ask, "If you say, 'I am a child of God,' how do you feel?" He then would tell me that he felt restful. Based on this, I would point out to him that he had the assurance within and that this was sufficient to prove that he was a child of God.

It means nothing for others to bear outward witness that we are children of God. However, we have an inner witness which testifies that we are children of God, and nothing in the universe can ever take this away from us. The inner witness is personal and beyond human expression. The Holy Spirit of God is now in our spirit, bearing witness with our spirit. These two spirits work together as one to bear witness to the fact that we are children of God.

Once a brother who had committed a serious sin told me that he did not think he was a child of God. He thought that a child of God could never commit such a sin. I told him to declare that he was not a child of God and to tell this to God, to the angels, and even to Satan. He responded that he could not do this because something within him troubled him. He had to admit that he was a child of God. According to his mind, he thought that he was not a child of God, but another part of him gave him the sense that he was a child of God. Then I advised him to go along with God according to this other part.

We all have the inner assurance that we are children of God. This inner assurance is the witnessing of the Holy Spirit of God with our regenerated spirit. It is something very precious and wonderful, something that no one can take away. Therefore, Romans 8:16 is a verse that shows us the two spirits, the Spirit of God and our spirit, working together as one.

ONE SPIRIT WITH THE LORD

In 1 Corinthians 6:17 we see that the two spirits, the divine Spirit and the human spirit, become one spirit. This verse says, "But he who is joined to the Lord is one spirit." We must realize that today we are one spirit with the Lord. The Lord is Spirit, and we have a spirit. When the Lord Spirit came into our spirit to enliven our spirit and to regenerate our spirit with Christ as life, the two spirits, the Lord Spirit and our spirit, were mingled as one and were joined as one spirit. Since we are joined to the Lord, we are one spirit with Him. This is a wonderful, accomplished fact. On the day we were regenerated, we became one spirit with the Lord.

Furthermore, 1 Corinthians 15:45 says, "The first man, Adam, became a living soul; the last Adam became a life-giving Spirit." The last Adam undoubtedly is Christ. According to this verse Christ today, that is, Christ in resurrection, is a life-giving Spirit. The Christ who has entered into our spirit is the life-giving Spirit. He is a Spirit, and He enters into us to give life to our spirit. At the time that He enters into us, He joins Himself with our spirit and makes our spirit and Himself as the Spirit one spirit. The two spirits are mingled together as one.

Whereas Adam was a living soul, Christ is a life-giving Spirit. A living soul cannot give life to others. Christ is a Spirit who not only is living but also can give life to others. Hence, He is a life-giving Spirit, and when He comes into us, He gives us life. He enlivens our spirit, and He causes our spirit to be mingled with Himself as the Spirit. Our spirit and the Lord Spirit mingle together as one spirit, with the result that we become one spirit with the Lord.

The fact that the Lord is the Spirit is also clearly seen in 2 Corinthians 3:17, which says, "The Lord is the Spirit." Based on 1 Corinthians 15:45 alone we may think that Christ is only a life-giving Spirit, not the Holy Spirit. But the Spirit referred to in 2 Corinthians 3:17 is the Holy Spirit, the unique Spirit of God, the same Spirit as mentioned earlier in the chapter (vv. 3, 6, 8). From its beginning this chapter speaks much about the Holy Spirit, and in verse 17 it tells us that the Lord is the Spirit. Therefore, the Lord, who is Christ (4:5), is the Holy Spirit. We must realize that the Holy Spirit is simply the Lord Christ Himself. We should not think that the Holy Spirit and the Lord Christ are two separate persons. According to the pure word of the Scriptures, Christ and the Holy Spirit are one.

The second part of 2 Corinthians 3:17, and verse 18, continue, "Where the Spirit of the Lord is, there is freedom. But we all with unveiled face, beholding and reflecting like a mirror the glory of the Lord, are being transformed into the same image from glory to glory, even as from the Lord Spirit." On the one hand, the second part of verse 17 refers to the Spirit as "the Spirit of the Lord," and on the other hand, verse 18 refers to the Spirit as "the Lord Spirit." These two titles both confirm that the Lord Himself is the Spirit. According to verse 18, we can be transformed into the image of the Lord by the Lord Spirit, and this Spirit is the Lord Himself. This indicates that we can be transformed into the image of the Lord only by the Lord Himself, who is the Spirit.

We need to be concerned about two things. The first thing is that God is Spirit. In order to worship Him, to contact Him, we must exercise our spirit. We must contact God and worship Him in our spirit. The second thing is that we have a spirit, and this spirit has been enlivened and regenerated by the Lord. Today the Lord Himself is in our spirit, and we are one spirit with Him.

If we are asked where the Lord is today, we should answer not only that He is in us but also that He is in our spirit (2 Tim. 4:22). To say that the Lord is in the heavens is to answer from the standpoint of the universe. As far as we are concerned, the Lord is within us, and He is not merely within us; He is also in our spirit. As regenerated persons, we must locate the Lord within us. We need to be simple and realize that we are regenerated persons with a regenerated spirit, and the Lord is now in our spirit and is one spirit with us. We should forget about everything else. If we do this, we will know the Lord in a much more definite way.

THE THREE PARTS OF MAN

We also need to see what our spirit is and what the difference is between our spirit and our mind, emotion, will, and heart. We will consider a number of verses which show that the spirit is different from the soul.

First Thessalonians 5:23 says, "The God of peace Himself sanctify you wholly, and may your spirit and soul and body be preserved complete, without blame, at the coming of our Lord Jesus Christ." This verse speaks of the three parts of man: spirit, soul, and body. We should not think that our spirit is the same as our soul. A number of Christians have a wrong concept, thinking that the soul and the spirit are the same. In this verse, however, the three parts of man are conjoined by *and:* spirit *and* soul *and* body. Hence, just as the soul is different from the body, so the spirit is different from both the soul and the body. The spirit, the soul, and the body are three different things. Furthermore, the sequence in the verse is first the spirit, then the soul, and then the body. The spirit is the innermost part, the body is the outermost part, and the soul is in the middle as a medium between the spirit and the body. Thus, God is triune and man is tripartite.

This is also quite clear when we consider our experience. As far as man is concerned, there are at least three different realms. There is the physical, material realm with many material things. There is also the spiritual realm with the spiritual things. In this realm are God, God's angels, the devil Satan, and his servants the evil spirits. All these belong to the spiritual realm. Besides the physical and the spiritual realms, there is another realm, which we may call the psychological realm. The English word *psychology* comes from the Greek word *psuche,* which means "soul." Thus, the psychological realm is the realm of the soul.

Not only are there three realms, but God has created three parts for us that we may contact these three realms. The part we use to contact the physical realm is the body with its five senses, and the part we use to contact the spiritual realm is our human spirit. We cannot contact the spiritual realm by using our hand to touch it; we must contact it by our spirit. For an object in the physical realm, we need to use our eyes to see it and our hands to touch it. To try to touch a physical object by using our mind is to use the wrong organ. When we are happy, joyful, or angry, this is psychological, not spiritual. The God who is both in the universe and in us is neither physical nor psychological. God is Spirit; hence, He is related to the spiritual realm.

Genesis 2:7 says, "Jehovah God formed man from the dust of the ground and breathed into his nostrils the breath of life, and man became a living soul." Here also we can see the three parts of man. First, there was man's body, formed from the dust of the ground. Then there was man's spirit, formed by God from the breath of life breathed out of God and into man's body (cf. Prov. 20:27; Job 32:8). When these two came together, that is, when the breath of life animated man's body, a third part came into being, which was the soul as the medium between the spirit and the body.

THE TWO PERSONS WITHIN US

The person of man is neither the body nor the spirit. Rather, man's person is his soul, because "man became a living soul." In the Scriptures persons are often called "souls." For example, Exodus 1:5 says, "All the souls who came forth from the loins of Jacob were seventy souls" (lit.). We all are souls. Our body is not our person; it is a vessel to contain our soul. Our spirit also is not our person but is an organ by which we can contact the spiritual realm. Our person, or personality, is in our soul, for the soul is the self, the person himself. When a man dies, we say that he has departed and is no longer with us. What we mean is that he has left his body, which can be put off like a piece of clothing (2 Cor. 5:4). Therefore, neither the body nor the spirit is the person of man. The body is the vessel, and the spirit is an organ. The soul is the person, the personality, and the self of man.

However, as we have seen, through regeneration our spirit has been not only enlivened but also born. In our spirit there is now another person. Before we were regenerated, our spirit was merely an organ, not a person, but now that we are regenerated, our spirit is both an organ and a person. Another life, a second life, has come into our spirit, and this life is the life of God, which is Christ Himself. Christ as a person is now in our spirit (2 Tim. 4:22).

Before our regeneration we as created beings had only one person. Our personality was in our soul, which was our self, our very being. Our body was a vessel to contain our soul, and our spirit was an organ to contact God. Hence, we had just one person, one being, one personality. But once we are regenerated and the Lord Jesus as life has come into our spirit, we have another person, another life, in our spirit. Now there are two persons within us—a spiritual person and a soulish, natural person. Second Corinthians 4:16 clearly indicates that there are two men, or two persons: "Therefore we do not lose heart; but though our outer man is decaying, yet our inner man is being renewed day by day." *Decaying* in this verse means "being wasted away." Our outer man is being wasted away, and our inner man is being renewed day by day. Through creation we became a soul, but our soul was damaged by the fall of man and fell under the control of the fallen body, which has become the flesh. Therefore, on the one hand, the Scriptures call man a soul, and on the other hand, they refer to man as "flesh" (Gen. 6:3; Rom. 3:20). This is because man has fallen to the point that he is absolutely under the control of his fleshly body, causing his soul to become fleshly.

We need to see that now we have two persons within us, the outer man and the inner man, because we have two lives, the natural, human life, and the spiritual, divine life. We have all been born twice, the first time of our parents to receive the natural, human life, and the second time of God to receive the spiritual, divine life.

Moreover, with each of these lives there is a nature and a person. As regenerated ones, we have two lives, two natures, and two persons. Our first person is in our soul, and our second person is in our spirit. For this reason 1 Corinthians 2:14-15 says, "A soulish man does not receive the things of the Spirit of God, for they are foolishness to him and he is not able to know them because they are discerned spiritually. But the spiritual man discerns all things, but he himself is discerned by no one." These verses show two kinds of men, the soulish man and the spiritual man. Since we have two persons and are thus two different men, we are faced with two possibilities: we can be either a natural, soulish man or a spiritual man. If we live by our natural human life, we are a natural man, a soulish man, but if we live by our spirit, we are a spiritual man.

We have seen clearly that God created us as a soul, with a body as the vessel to contain the soul and with a spirit as the organ to contact God. As created men, we were merely a soul, a soulish personality, a soulish man. However, on the day that we received the Lord Jesus, He came into our spirit as life to regenerate our spirit and cause it to be born again. Now in our spirit we have a second life—Christ as the second man (1 Cor. 15:47). As a result, we now have two men within us. In our soul we have Adam, and in our spirit we have Christ; in our soul we have the soulish nature, character, and personality, that is, the soulish man, and in our spirit we have the spiritual nature, character, and personality, that is, the spiritual man.

WALKING BY THE SPIRIT AS SPIRITUAL MEN

Now we need to consider practically what person we are living by today. Are we living by the first person or by the second, by the soul or by the spirit? If we live by the soul, we are soulish men, but if we live by the spirit, we are spiritual men.

Although the soul represents our whole being, it is only one part of our being. The soul is composed of three parts: the mind, the emotion, and the will (Prov. 2:10; Psa. 139:14; 1 Sam. 18:1; Job 7:15). We have a mind to think, to consider, and we have an emotion to love and to hate, to like and to dislike, and to be happy, angry, and sorrowful. We also have a will with which to make decisions. However, we have a spirit that is deeper than our soul. Often when we are about to do something, we first consider whether it is reasonable and right to do. This reasoning is according to our mind. Then in our emotion we may like it and desire to do it. Following this, our will makes the decision to do it. However, while we are making the decision, we sense that something within us that is deeper than our mind, emotion, and will is protesting against what we want and intend to do. This is the innermost part of our being, our spirit. Hence, our experience confirms that besides our soul there is another part within us, our spirit, which is deeper than our mind, our emotion, and our will.

As regenerated Christians, we should live, walk, and do things by our spirit, not by our mind, our emotion, or our will (Rom. 8:4; Gal. 5:16). To live by the mind, the emotion, and the will is to live by the soul, and to live by the soul is to live by the old self, the old man. Sadly, many Christians today still live and walk by the old self, the soulish man, the soul-life, the natural self, that is, the soul with its mind, emotion, and will. Instead of living by the soul, we should live by the spirit, which is much deeper than the mind, the emotion, and the will.

In order to live by the spirit, we need to see that the old man, the soulish life and nature, and the self have been crucified (Rom. 6:6; Gal. 2:20). As believers, we must realize the fact that our old man has been put on the cross and has thus been put to death, terminated. We should not allow this dead old man to come alive again. The Lord said in Matthew 16:24, "If anyone wants to come after Me, let him deny himself and take up his cross and follow Me." Here the Lord Jesus told us that if we want to follow Him, we must deny the self, the soul, the old man. Since the Lord has put the old man on the cross, we must bear the cross. On the one hand, we must keep ourselves on the cross and not put the cross away; on the other hand, we must deny our self. Actually, to bear the cross is simply to deny our self, because the cross has put us, the old man, to death. We need to recognize this fact and apply to our self, our old man, and our old nature what the Lord has accomplished on the cross. In other words, we must reject the old man absolutely and not live by the old man, that is, by the mind, the emotion, or the will. Instead, we should simply follow the Lord by the spirit, walking in our spirit and according to our spirit. If we live in such a way, we are spiritual men.

In order to live and walk according to the spirit, we need to discern between the soul and the spirit, between the old man and the new man, between the natural life and the spiritual life, and between the self and Christ. Hebrews 4:12 speaks of this discernment: "For the word of God is living and operative and sharper than any two-edged sword, and piercing even to the dividing of soul and spirit and of joints and marrow, and able to discern the thoughts and intentions of the heart." Our spirit must be clearly divided from our soul. As Christians, we need to discern what is of our spirit and what is of our soul, because we need to reject the soul. We must realize that our old man, our self, our natural life, has been crucified. The old man is the soul, and the self is the natural life. We must divide what is of the spirit from all the things that are of the soul so that we can reject the soul. This is to deny the self and apply the cross to our old man, that is, to bear the cross by keeping the old man continually on the cross.

Many Christians today have the mistaken concept that to bear the cross is to suffer. In actual fact, however, the cross is not merely for us to suffer but for us to be put to death, terminated. We must realize that we have already been put to an end and that our self, the old man, is good for nothing other than to be crucified. The Lord has put this old man on the cross, and we should simply recognize this and leave him there. This is the correct meaning of bearing the cross. We must learn to bear the cross, to continually put our old man, our self, our natural life, to death by denying and rejecting it and living by the spirit. Then we will be spiritual men.

In the foregoing chapters we have seen how to apply and experience Christ and how to have a church life to realize the Body of Christ. In reality, the only way to experience Christ is in the spirit, and the only way to have a church life to realize the Body of Christ also is in the spirit. We must live, walk, and do things in the spirit. Then we will truly experience Christ, and it will be possible to realize the Body of Christ. We will have a genuine church life by living, walking, and conducting ourselves in the spirit.

Chapter Eight

THE PRIESTHOOD

Scripture Reading: Exo. 19:6; 1 Pet. 2:5, 9; Rev. 1:5b-6, 9; 20:6; 22:3

GOD'S INTENTION AND THE PRIESTHOOD

In this universe God has an administration, in which is His divine economy. The Greek word for *economy* means "household law," implying a plan, an administration, an arrangement, for distributing, or dispensing, the household supply to the members of a family. The base of this word is of the same origin as that for *pasture* in John 10:9, implying a distribution of the pasture to the flock. God's economy is His household economy, His household administration (Eph. 1:10; 3:9; 1 Tim. 1:4), which is to dispense Himself in Christ into His chosen people that He may have a house to express Himself, which house is the church (3:15), the Body of Christ. In God's economy, in this divine household administration, there are three main ministries: the priesthood, the kingship, and the prophethood. The priesthood is the first and leading ministry in God's economy.

In the New Testament three Greek words are used in relation to the priesthood. The first word refers to the priestly office, as in Hebrews 7:12; the second refers to the priestly service, as in Hebrews 7:5; and the third refers to the assembly of priests, a priesthood, a body of priests who serve in a corporate way, as in 1 Peter 2:5 and 9. According to the natural human concept, a priest is a professional person, a person whose profession is to serve God. Most Christians consider a priest to be someone who serves God. Although this is correct, it is necessary to explain what it means to serve God. The common concept among Christians is that to serve God is to work for God. However, this is not an accurate concept. Although it is right to say that a priest is a person who serves God, it is wrong to consider that to serve God is merely to do something for God or to work for God.

In order to know what it means to be a priest, we must first discover God's eternal intention, that is, God's desire in eternity past and His intention for eternity future. God is a God of purpose. Just as we human beings are purposeful and always do things with a purpose, God, who is much greater than we are, is a God of purpose who has an intention to accomplish.

The Scriptures reveal that before the ages, in eternity past before the foundation of the world, God had a good pleasure, a heart's desire (Eph. 1:9). According to His good pleasure, He made a purpose, an intention, to gain His heart's desire, and He also made a plan to accomplish His purpose (3:11). In this plan He determined to work Himself into a group of people so that He might be their life and they might be His expression (1:5). Based on this divine determination, God created man. Man was destined to receive God, to be filled with God, to be saturated and permeated with God, and even to flow God out, so that he might be the living expression of God (Gen. 1:26; 2:8-10; John 7:37-39; Eph. 3:19; 1:22-23).

Although a priest is a person who serves God, this does not mean that he works for God and does something for God. According to the revelation of the Scriptures, to serve God is to receive God into us, to contact God, and to be filled with God, saturated with God, and permeated with God. Furthermore, to serve God is to flow God out and, in this flow of God, to be built up with others as a corporate expression of God. This is the proper meaning of serving God and of being a priest. A priest is simply a person who is filled with God, one with God, taken over by God, and even possessed by God in a full way and built up with others in the flow of the life of God to be a living, corporate expression of God on earth today. This built-up corporate entity is the priesthood.

THE PRIESTHOOD AND THE FLOW OF GOD

In Christianity there is the concept that if we love God and fear Him, we must work for Him. According to this concept we must consecrate ourselves to the Lord so that we may be His servants who do His will, serving Him by working for Him. But this is actually a natural, religious concept, not a revelation from the heavens. God has no intention whatsoever of calling us simply to work for Him or to do something for Him. Rather, God's intention is for us to open ourselves to Him. We should not do anything for God but should open ourselves to Him so that He may come into us, fill us, and even flood us. In this way God will saturate us, permeate us, take us over, and take possession of every part of our being. When our whole being is taken over by Him, possessed by Him, and saturated and permeated with Him, we will be one with Him. Indeed, we will be full of Him, not only by being outwardly clothed with Him as power but also by being inwardly permeated with Him as everything to us. We will be God-men, persons full of God, and spontaneously God will flow Himself out of us. Moreover, in this flow of God, which is the flow of life, we will be built up with others.

People who are swept away in a flood can never be independent. They are carried along in the one flow of the flood waters. If we are all on dry land, it will be very easy for us to be independent and individualistic. But if a flood comes and sweeps us away in its current, we will all lose our independence and individualism. We will all be "one" in the flood, for we will be carried along in one direction. It will not matter whether or not we agree to go in the direction of the flood. We will have no choice but to go in the same direction. We may disagree with one another, but we will have no way to disagree with the flood. Likewise, when we are one with God and are in the flow of God, we will be one with one another and will be built up together in this one flow. The final picture in the Bible shows a river of water of life proceeding out of the throne of God and of the Lamb and flowing through the whole city of New Jerusalem (Rev. 22:1-2). The whole city is in the one flow. This is a picture of the priesthood.

The Principal Service of a Priest

I must repeat that to be a priest is not merely to work for God. We must forget about this kind of concept. When I was

young, I considered that a servant of the Lord was a priest
who served the Lord full time, and I thought that a servant of
the Lord should endeavor, struggle, and strive to do something
for the Lord. One day the Lord opened my eyes to see that my
concept was wrong. God has no intention to call us to do something for Him. His unique intention is for us to answer His
call by opening ourselves to Him and telling Him, "Lord, here
I am. I am ready not to do something for You or to work for
You but to be filled and even be taken over by You so that I
may be fully possessed by You and with You. I am ready to
be one with You." Until we are one with the Lord, we can do
nothing for Him; we can neither work for Him nor be a genuine priest.

Furthermore, we must see that the main work and conduct
of the priests is not to offer sacrifices but to spend time in the
presence of the Lord to be filled, saturated, and permeated by
and with the Lord until they are one with Him in the spirit.
Before spending time with the Lord and being saturated with
Him, they can never be adequate priests. A priest is not a
person who does something for God but a person who is filled
with God. This is a priest, and this is the man God planned to
have. God planned to have a corporate man who would not be
engaged in doing something for Him but who would be filled
with Him. If we have this light, we will realize that every man
should be a priest, one who receives God and opens himself to
God to be filled with God and to be saturated, permeated, and
possessed wholly, fully, and thoroughly by and with God.

SOME EXAMPLES OF THE PRIESTHOOD IN THE BIBLE

Adam

We have pointed out that the priesthood is not any kind of
service in which we do something or work for God. The priesthood is a group of persons who are filled with God, saturated
and permeated by and with God, and one with God, and out of
whom God Himself is flowing. These people become a corporate Body as a corporate expression of God.

In the Bible the first priest was not Aaron but Adam.
When Adam was in the garden of Eden, he had no sin and

thus did not need to offer sacrifices for sin. This indicates that to be a priest is not merely a matter of offering sacrifices to God. Even though Adam did not need to offer any sacrifices before the fall, he was continually in the presence of God. After creating man, God did not place any demand on man. Instead, He put him in front of the tree of life (Gen. 2:8-9). This portrays God's desire that Adam would spend time in the presence of God, enjoying God Himself as the tree of life. Adam did not need to do anything for God; he only needed to take God in again and again as food, as his life and life supply, so that he would be filled with God and be full of the elements of God. Then he would be saturated and permeated by and with God. However, Adam failed in this matter.

The Priests in the Tabernacle and the Temple

After God had delivered the children of Israel out of Egypt and had brought them to Mount Sinai, He spoke to Moses and said, "Now therefore if you will indeed obey My voice and keep My covenant, then you shall be My personal treasure from among all peoples, for all the earth is Mine. And you shall be to Me a kingdom of priests and a holy nation. These are the words that you shall speak to the children of Israel" (Exo. 19:5-6). This word spoken by God indicates that God ordained the entire nation of Israel to be a kingdom of priests. This means that God wanted all the children of Israel to be priests. However, because they worshipped the golden calf (32:1-6), they lost the priesthood, and only the tribe of Levi, because of its faithfulness to God, was chosen to replace the whole nation of Israel as priests to God (vv. 25-29; Deut. 33:8-10). The family of Aaron of the tribe of Levi became the priests who served God in the tabernacle and the temple, and the rest of the Levites served under them.

The priests who served in the tabernacle and the temple offered sacrifices in the outer court, but that was only a part of their service. The work of the priests in offering the sacrifices was somewhat coarse and rough. The animals had to be slain, and certain parts of their bodies, with the blood, had to be offered on the altar. After finishing their work at the altar, the priests entered the Holy Place to do a much finer work.

In the Holy Place they spread the bread on the table, lit the lamps, and burned the incense on the golden altar. All of these items—the bread, the shining of the light, and the incense of sweet odor—are related to the finer experiences of Christ. Day by day we need to deal with all these finer experiences. We must not only shout, cry, and offer the sacrifices in a coarse, rough way; we must also deal with the finer experiences of Christ in the Holy Place. Nevertheless, there is something deeper still. After completing his service in the Holy Place, on certain occasions the high priest entered into the Holy of Holies. In the Holy of Holies there was very little for him to do. There he was quiet and calm, and all human activity ceased. This indicates that what the Lord needs is not our working for Him but our ceasing from work in order to be filled with Him.

Moses

In the same principle, when Moses spent forty days in the presence of Jehovah (Exo. 34), in reality he was in the Holy of Holies. He spent forty days without doing any kind of work, for the purpose of being filled with the Lord, saturated with the Lord, and being one with the Lord. Those forty days show us a real picture of a priest who was not in the outer court or in the Holy Place but in the Holy of Holies, that is, in the presence of God's shekinah glory. He was completely stopped from every kind of work and was absolutely open to God. As a result, he was filled, saturated, and permeated by and with God so that eventually he became one with God. When he came down from the mountain, the people saw the shekinah glory of God on his face. Because he was truly one with God, he was a real priest.

Other Old Testament Saints

We should not think, however, that there were no other priests in the Old Testament after the Levites. Although in a legal sense there were no other priests, in a spiritual sense many of the saints in the Old Testament were priests. For example, consider the psalmists who wrote the Psalms. When we read their writings, we realize that they were genuine priests because they spent much time in the presence of God. As a result, they were filled with God and occupied by and with God. Because they were one with God, they could express God in a living way and also in a corporate way.

The New Testament Apostles

In the New Testament the apostles also were genuine priests, persons who opened themselves to the Lord. They were filled with the Lord and saturated with the Lord, and so they were truly one with the Lord and were the expression of the Lord in a corporate way. According to the teaching of the New Testament, all the believers should be this kind of person. Both the apostle Peter and the apostle John told us that we are priests and are corporately the priesthood (1 Pet. 2:5, 9; Rev. 1:5b-6, 9; 20:6; 22:3).

Our concept concerning the priesthood needs to be transformed, adjusted, and changed. To serve God is not mainly to do something for the Lord or work for Him, but to be taken over by the Lord. We must spend time, more time, and even all our time in the presence of the Lord to open ourselves that He may come in and flood us, that is, fill us, saturate us, and even permeate our entire being.

THE PRIESTHOOD AND THE BUILDING UP OF THE CHURCH

When I began to serve the Lord, I liked to talk with people about working for the Lord. Now I have no appetite for this because I have seen that it is not a matter of working for the Lord but a matter of being filled with Him, taken over by Him, possessed by Him, and saturated and permeated by and with Him. Serving the Lord is a matter of spending time in the presence of His shekinah glory. Then He will flow Himself out of us, and that flow will be our real work and service. This flow of God out of us is the very thing that we must take care of, for it is uniquely this that fulfills the Lord's purpose. It is not a matter of working in this or that way; it is not a matter of method, form, or any kind of teaching or gift. Rather, it is a matter of being filled and possessed by the Lord and of being fully, thoroughly, and wholly permeated by and with Him. Then we will become one with Him, and there will be a certain flow out of us all the time. In this flow we are one not only with God but also with all the other members of the Body. In this flow we have our work and service to the Lord, the church life, the Body life, and the building up of the Body. The building up of the Body is not a work, nor is it any kind of organization. It is a corporate life in the flow of God Himself.

Therefore, we all must be filled with God, taken over by Him, possessed by Him, and saturated and permeated with His shekinah glory. Then we will be one with Him, and we will be one with one another in His flow. This is the testimony, the recovery, and the building up of the church. This is also the service, and this must be the preaching of the gospel. All Christian work and service, the building of the church, and the reaching out to others must come forth from this priesthood. God has absolutely no intention in this age for us to do something for Him. His heart's desire is that we would be fully open to Him and allow Him to fill us. For this we must spend adequate time in His presence, allowing Him take us over, possess us, and even saturate us with Himself. This is the priesthood, and this is the kind of person God planned to have and desires to have today.

The following hymn helps us to realize that for the building of the church, there is a great need today for such a priesthood, for such a group of people who know God in this way.

> What a blessing, what a priv'lege!
>   Called of God a royal priest,
>   That this glorious, holy office
>   I should bear, though last and least.
>
> All the building of the Body
>   On the priesthood doth depend;
>   Ever praying in the spirit
>   I this office would attend.
>
> If I keep this royal calling
>   Under Thine authority,
>   Priestly duty thus fulfilling,
>   Then the church will builded be.

Now the church is but the priesthood;
　　Thus the priesthood formed we need;
When the priests are knit together,
　　Then the church is built indeed.

Through the church's degradation,
　　Saints this office desolate;
Through the weakness of their spirits
　　Preaching doth predominate.

Most are leaning on the message
　　And the preaching emphasize,
Yet neglect the priestly praying
　　And their spirits' exercise.

Deal with me and make me balanced,
　　As in preaching, so in prayer;
Leading others oft in praying,
　　As Thy Word I too declare.

Only serving by our praying
　　Will our spirits mingled be;
Stressing prayer as much as preaching—
　　Thus the church is built for Thee.

Hymns, #848

OTHER BOOKS PUBLISHED BY
Living Stream Ministry

Titles by Witness Lee:

Abraham—Called by God	0-7363-0359-6
The Experience of Life	0-87083-417-7
The Knowledge of Life	0-87083-419-3
The Tree of Life	0-87083-300-6
The Economy of God	0-87083-415-0
The Divine Economy	0-87083-268-9
God's New Testament Economy	0-87083-199-2
The World Situation and God's Move	0-87083-092-9
Christ vs. Religion	0-87083-010-4
The All-inclusive Christ	0-87083-020-1
Gospel Outlines	0-87083-039-2
Character	0-87083-322-7
The Secret of Experiencing Christ	0-87083-227-1
The Life and Way for the Practice of the Church Life	0-87083-785-0
The Basic Revelation in the Holy Scriptures	0-87083-105-4
The Crucial Revelation of Life in the Scriptures	0-87083-372-3
The Spirit with Our Spirit	0-87083-798-2
Christ as the Reality	0-87083-047-3
The Central Line of the Divine Revelation	0-87083-960-8
The Full Knowledge of the Word of God	0-87083-289-1
Watchman Nee—A Seer of the Divine Revelation ...	0-87083-625-0

Titles by Watchman Nee:

How to Study the Bible	0-7363-0407-X
God's Overcomers	0-7363-0433-9
The New Covenant	0-7363-0088-0
The Spiritual Man 3 volumes	0-7363-0269-7
Authority and Submission	0-7363-0185-2
The Overcoming Life	1-57593-817-0
The Glorious Church	0-87083-745-1
The Prayer Ministry of the Church	0-87083-860-1
The Breaking of the Outer Man and the Release ...	1-57593-955-X
The Mystery of Christ	1-57593-954-1
The God of Abraham, Isaac, and Jacob	0-87083-932-2
The Song of Songs	0-87083-872-5
The Gospel of God 2 volumes	1-57593-953-3
The Normal Christian Church Life	0-87083-027-9
The Character of the Lord's Worker	1-57593-322-5
The Normal Christian Faith	0-87083-748-6
Watchman Nee's Testimony	0-87083-051-1

Available at
Christian bookstores, or contact Living Stream Ministry
2431 W. La Palma Ave. • Anaheim, CA 92801
1-800-549-5164 • www.livingstream.com